ECONOMIC EMPOWERMENT OF WOMEN THROUGH SELF-HELP GROUPS

ECONOMIC EMPOWERMENT OF WOMEN THROUGH SELF-HELP GROUPS

By

Dr. P. Sindhuja

DPH

DISCOVERY PUBLISHING HOUSE PVT. LTD.
NEW DELHI-110 002

Published by:
Tilak Wasan
DISCOVERY PUBLISHING HOUSE PVT. LTD.
4831/24, Ansari Road, Prahlad Street
Darya Ganj, New Delhi-110002 (India)
Phone: +91-11-23279245, 43764432
Fax: +91-11-23253475
E-mail: parul.wasan@gmail.com
info@discoverypublishinggroup.com
web: www.discoverypublishinggroup.com

First Edition: **2011**
ISBN: 978-81-8356-726-8

Economic Empowerment of Women Through Self-Help Groups

PREFACE

Women constitute half of the population and among them, only one-fourth are contributing effectively for the economic development of the country. The human resources among the women could not be utilized effectively due to illiteracy, low education and lack of skills. Most women workers in India are engaged in agriculture, where livelihood is insecure and wages are low. Recognizing that women can leverage their strength, increase bargaining power and enhance capacities and skills through joint action, the government has approved to organize women into groups and chanellized the resources to these groups.

Self-Help Groups (SHGs) are usually informal groups whose members have a common perception of need and importance towards collective action. These group promote savings among members and used the pooled resources to meet the emergent needs of their members. The number of members in SHGs is normally ranged from 10 to 20. SHGs aims at empowering women and thus uplifting their families above the poverty line. It targets the rural and urban households below the poverty line and assure the poor women employment and income.

The study sample was women SHG beneficiaries in Andhra Pradesh and Kerala. The study is presented in six chapters. The study opens with the Introduction in Chapter 1. Review of literature was presented in detail in Chapter 2. Chapter 3 gives the statement of problems, objectives and hypotheses. Methodology comprising of sampling, variables and their empirical measurements and the statistical methods used in the study was presented in Chapter 4. Chapter 5 deals with Results and Discussion. Summary and conclusions were presented in Chapter VI.

The study is useful for the students of Social Sciences and for field counselors, Sociologists, Social workers and for voluntary agencies.

Dr. P. SINDHUJA

ACKNOWLEDGEMENTS

I am greatly indebted to my Research Supervisor Prof. (Mrs.) V. Sreedevi, Professor, Department of Home Science, S.V. University, Tirupati without whose help the work would not have taken this shape. I am enlightened myself with her thorough discussions, critical analysis and bright ideas in executing my day-to-day work. She has taken a lot of interest in giving timely suggestions for the completion of this work. I express my heartful thanks and indebtedness to my guide for her perseverance, encouragement, coherent thinking, cooperation and critical evaluation extended to me during the progress of the work.

I express my deep sense of gratitude to Prof. (Mrs.) D. Usha Rani, Director, Centre for Extension Studies, S.V. University, Tirupati, for her valuable suggestions, cooperation, critical evaluation and support which helped me a lot throughout the period of my research investigation.

My sincere thanks are due to Prof. D. Baby, Former Head and Prof. V. Kalavathi, Head of the Department of Home Science, for providing me the necessary facilities during my research work.

I am also grateful to the Project Officials, Mr. Gopa Kumar, Asst. B.D.O., Ottapalam, Kerala, Mr. Bharathan and Mrs. Geetha, Community Organisers, Ottapalam, and Mr. Malleswar Reddy and Mr. Umesh Rao,

Community Organisers, Madanapalle, DWCRA Officials for giving permission and cooperation.

I am very much thankful to Prof. K.V. Sharma, Department of Statistics, Sri Venkateswara University, Tirupati for his co-operative and cheerful assistance in the statistical analysis.

I express my sincere thanks to all the respondents of the study who cheerfully cooperated and helped me in carrying out the investigation successfully.

I am also thankful to the library authorities of NIRD, Hyderabad, Kerala Agricultural University, Thrissur, Mahila University, Tirupati, ANGRAU, Tirupati, S.V. University for giving permission to use their respective libraries.

Diction is not enough to express my unboundful gratitude and regards from my inner corner of the heart to my ever beloved parents

Late Sri P. Govindan Nair and Smt. A. P. Kamalakshi-amma without whose affection, encouragement and moral support, I would not have been in this stage.

I take the opportunity to express my profound sense of love and gratitude to all my brothers, sisters, sister-in-laws and brother-in-laws for their constant help through out the period of this investigation.

I am in dearth of words to express my deep sense of gratitude to my husband Mr. K. K. Ramachandran for his unstinted patience, encouragement, cooperation and providing me moral and spiritual strength. Indeed I should spell a word of thanks to my daughter S.R. Amrita for allowing me to write this thesis.

My diction of thanks will be in commensurate to my friends Dr. M. Syamala Devi and Dr. K. Latha Reddy, for their support and cooperation.

I owe my profound thanks to Dr. R. K. Anuradha, Associate Professor, Department of Home Science, S.V. University, Tirupati for her constant encouragement and moral support.

Last but not least, I thank students, for typing the work judiciously and expeditiously

Dr. P. SINDHUJA

CONTENTS

CHAPTER 1

INTRODUCTION

The Nobel scholar and Indian economist Mr. Amartya Sen expressed in his words "Unless women are empowered, issues like literacy, health, population explosion etc. will remain unresolved problems of the developing countries". Majority of the women in India still continue to perform their traditional roles in the household and in agriculture. But the 73rd amendment to the Constitution highlighting the importance of women's participation at the gross-root level in community decision making process is gaining importance. The development reports that UNDP published annually, have declared that women's empowerment is not merely important but crucial if development is to be sustainable. In a developing society, women in particular and more specifically rural poor and illiterate never get portrayed as agent at change. In almost all plans for poverty alleviation and social change, this subset of disadvantaged women became a target in development activities, rather than a group to be co-opted as active participants.

The International Conferences sponsored by the United Nations starting from Rio through Vienna, Copenhagen and Beijing have generated a lot of interest on the social development and highlighted the growing feminization of poverty and possible impact on women of the structural adjustment process. The preface to the platform for action adopted by the Fourth World Conference on Women held in Beijing 1995, revealed that women's empowerment and their full co-operation on the basis of equity in all spheres of society are fundamental for the achievement of equity, development and peace. The world micro credit summit held in Washington has realized that there were 10 million women who were organized into Self-help Groups (SHGs). Grameen Bank of Bangladesh, SEWA of Gujarat, Indian working women's forum of Tamil Nadu were some of the major initiatives which were attempting to address the gigantic issues of poverty eradication.

The Self-help Groups were viable alternatives to achieve the objectives of rural development and to get community participation in all the rural development programmes. SHG is an organizational setup to disburse micro-credit to the women for the purpose of making them enterprising women and encouraging them to enter into entrepreneurial activities. The women led SHGs have successfully demonstrated how to mobilize and manage thrift and credit needs, maintain linkages with the banks and enforce financial self-discipline. Today there are 4,75,446 self-help groups with 65,39,821 women members in the country progressing in the development sector with micro credit funding in India amounting to 174.65 crore. Out of the total SHG members, 68% are engaged in primary sector, 9% in secondary and 23% in tertiary sector.

It has been experienced during the implementation of DWCRA groups that poor women beneficiaries always feel the need for funds to carry economic activity. As such Government of India has taken up an innovative theme of women's empowerment as one of the main agenda items to tackle poverty and socio economic crisis. Self–help Group movement (SHGM) through savings had been taken up as a mass movement by the women to shape their future destiny.

EMPOWERMENT OF WOMEN THROUGH SHGs

Mahatma Gandhi states that the position of women in the society is an index of its civilization. "Train a man and you train an individual, Train a woman and you build a nation". The SHGs are the major resource of inspiration for women's welfare. In an attempt to uplifting the women, the government has initiated Women Welfare Programmes through development centers, rural agencies, banks, NABARD etc. In India, most of the SHGs are lead by woman with benefits of socio-economic homogeneity smaller size, functionality, participation, voluntary operating mode and non political women. The SHGs in India operating from April 1999, have entered into various fields like dairy farms, fisheries, ration shops, handlooms, farm cultivation, rain water harvesting etc.

Special programmes have been designed for training and capacity building of women beneficiaries of the SHGs. Regular skill development training programmes are being organized for value addition to DWCRA and SHGs productions for better packaging, standardization of ingredients, pricing and to develop marketing skills among women. Women are exposed to best and relevant technologies displayed at training and technology development centers (TTDCs) in all districts.

The concept of SHGs moulds women as a responsible citizen of the country with social and economic status. It leads women to develop the habit of raising loans, form savings, inculcated with a sense of belongingness, habit of thrift and discipline among themselves. Groups actively take part in social welfare programmes focusing on dowry, AIDS awareness, nutrition, legal literacy, multiple roles of women and poverty alleviation programmes. The concept of self-monitoring has been introduced by the SHGs in a phased manner with the aim to make women totally own their movement and institutionalize its sustainability through networking. The women groups have taken the initiative to educate their own members with great enthusiasm. Women belonging to lowest strata of the society are getting habituated to savings and paved the way for decision making power in the family. In a developed country like India, SHGs uplift the women who are mostly invisible in the social structure by creating self-confidence and self-reliance.

CONCEPTUALIZATION OF EMPOWERMENT

Women are an integral part of every economy. Allround development and harmonious growth of a nation would be possible only when women are considered as equal partners in progress with men. However, in most developing countries, women have a low socio and economic status. In such countries effective empowerment of women is essential to harness the women labour in the main stream of economic development.

Empowerment is the process of enabling or authorizing an individual to think, behave, take action and central work in an autonomous way. It is the process by which one can gain control over one's destiny and the circumstances of their lives. Empowerment can be viewed as means of creating a social environment in which one can make decisions and make choices either individually or collectively for social transformation.

Women empowerment enables autonomy and control over their lives. The empowered women become agents of their own development, able to exercise choices to set their own agenda and be strong enough to challenge their subordinate position in the society.

Although women constitute half of world's population yet they are the largest group which is excluded from the benefits of social and economic development. Women constitute a strong labour force which needs to be mobilized and encouraged to make an effective contribution to the development process. In India, the work participation rate for women is less than half that of men. Despite efforts made towards economic empowerment of women, majority of the active female population continue to be confined to micro, small scale enterprises and the informal sector.

The Ninth Five-year Plan (1992-2002) adopted the strategy of women's component plan under which not less than 30 per cent of funds/benefits were earmarked for all the women-related sector's and women specific programmes.

The Tenth Five-year Plan (2002-07) also undertook steps to further strengthening of self-help groups and community based organizations for the empowerment of women. Special attention needs to be given to increasing employment opportunities and productive resources of women through special financial intermediaries, building women's competitiveness and increasing economic exchanges among women entrepreneurs.

The SHGs and micro-credit organizations have a long history. In Vietnam, *tontines* or *Hui* with 10-15 members involved in financial activities in cash or kind have been in existence for generations. In Indonesia, Credit unions, Fishermen groups, village-based bank like institutions, Irrigation groups etc., have been in existence since long. In Bangladesh, the success story of Grameen Bank is well-known (Pitt and Khandekar, 1998). Other countries like Thailand, Nepal, Sri Lanka and India have also initiated Self-help groups in uplifting the socio-economic conditions of poor, particularly women (Rekha, 2002).

In India, these self-help groups were promoted by NGOs, Banks and Co-operatives. The NABARD launched a pilot project for linking SHGs in February 1992. The Reserve Bank of India advises the commercial banks actively to participate in the linkage programme. Normally, after six months of existence of SHGs and after collecting a sufficient thrift fund, the groups approach the link banks (either commercial or co-operative) with its credit plan. The NABARD gives 100 per cent refinance to the Banks on their lending through SHGs.

ECONOMIC EMPOWERMENT OF WOMEN: THE CONCEPT AND APPROACH

Empowerment of women has become a subject of growing importance around the world in contemporary times. The concern is seen at different levels and circles which include government, bureaucracy, non-governmental organizations, researchers and women's empowerment. There has also been a shift in the demands of women from equality in 1970s to development in the 1980s to empowerment-social, political and economic since the 1990s. Since the term empowerment came in to be used from 80s. Empowerment of women has came to be accepted as a key objective of development. Empowerment is a process of improving women's control over resources, ideology and self. It is a process of enlarging the entitlements and choices of women.

Empowerment

The dictionary meaning of the word 'empowerment' is to give power to make them able (person/group). The *Oxford Dictionary* defines empowerment as the 'action of empowering, the state of being empowered'.

The term 'empowerment' as the range of activities from individual self-assertion to collective resistance, protest and mobilization that challenge basic power relations. Empowerment is a process aimed at changing the nature and directions of systematic forces, which marginalize women and other disadvantaged sections in a given context.

Economic Empowerment

Economic empowerment refers to earning power, collective bargaining for economic gains, control over means of production, involvement in decision-making regarding economic aspects of development of skills in management. Economic empowerment, implies a process of redistribution of resources and power between different groups. It helps in building confidence, self-assertion and courage.

Importance of Economic Empowerment

Poverty is the biggest challenge in India's development efforts to bring about a perceptible change in the quality of life of the people. In India, a vast section of its population suffers from malnutrition, unemployment, and poor health care. This is particularly, true in the case of four main weaker sections of society namely, women, children, scheduled castes and scheduled tribes. In rural India, the high rates of illiteracy and low economic status of women underlie the need for increasing their earning by providing income-generating assets. Provision of employment opportunities to rural women is one way to improve their nutrition, health, education and social status. In most of the developing countries greater emphasis is laid on the need for development of rural women and their active involvement in the main stream of development especially economic.

Group Strategy

In the context of absence of empowerment and given the vulnerability and powerlessness of women in the existing socio-economic set up, group strategies occupy considerable relevance. The formation of women's groups would be helpful to provide visibility and create micro level power pockets through sharing of ideas, skills and interactive capacity. Slowly women would learn to articulate their needs resulting in more appropriate participatory and grass-root level plans for them. It is also possible to cut across social barriers. Many groups in recent years have started crossing the barriers of religion and caste and working together harmoniously for economic betterment.

Poverty hits women the hardest. At the household, poor women skip a meal to facilitate the other members of the household to eat the little that is available. Women are greatly subjected to economic and social discrimination. Credit is not easily available to them. It would not be wrong to say that social empowerment would have little relevance without empowering them on the economic front. World Bank studies have shown that enhancement of women's earning would have a more profound effect on the welfare of the family as a whole. Since it increases women's income, it results more directly in better health and nutrition for children. Thus grouping women for economic empowerment is of great importance, which has major implications on the overall empowerment of women.

National Policy for Empowerment of Women

As a follow up action to the commitments made by India during the Fourth World Conference on Women held in Beijing during Sep. 1995. The Department of Women and Child Development has drafted a National Policy for the Empowerment of Women after nationwide consultations to enhance the status of women in all walks of life on par with men and actualize the constitutional guarantee of equality without discrimination on grounds of sex. In 1995 the draft policy was circulated to select women organizations for holding regional level consultations with State Governments, State Women Commissions, State Social Welfare Advisory Boards, Women's Organizations, Academicians, experts and activists.

EMPOWERMENT OF WOMEN IN ANDHRA PRADESH

The State of Andhra Pradesh, having more than ten million rural families (about 50 million individuals) has made an attempt in a similar direction and this has become one of the largest initiative in the world with four million women forming their own self-help groups. Under this initiative, the Government, the NGOs, the community based organizations and the civil society have come together to enable the poor to organize themselves into self-help groups with thrift as the entry point activity. Over 30 lakh women belonging to the weaker sections of the society, have become members of these self-help groups. Majority of them developed the habit of saving a Rupee a day, paving the way for socio-economic development. It is a paradoxical truth that nearly 40 per cent of the DWCRA groups in the country are available in Andhra Pradesh itself. During early 90s 10,000 groups have been formed and in the last five years there is tremendous increase in the DWCRA groups and 90,000 additional groups have been formed in the year 2000 alone.

Indira Kranthi Patham

The best political tribute to the SHGs came in 2004 when the newly installed Congress Government in Andhra Pradesh refined its commitment to Velugu, the

State government programme launched by the Former Chief Minister Mr. N. Chandra Babu Naidu with World Bank support in 2000 for promoting and operating SHGs by giving it an expanded role with a new name Indira Kranthi Patham (IKP). The IKP is managed by an independent society for the elimination of Rural Poverty (SERP) which is government agency with all the flexibility that a society structure provides administrative and managerial support to the entire SHG network.

EMPOWERMENT OF WOMEN - KERALA

Kerala is a State with an impressive array of achievements in the field of women development. It has a high female literacy rate of 86.2% a low IMR of 13 (against the average of 80) a favourable sex ratio of 1032 female/1000 male, high life expectancy ratio 74 female/70 male etc., just to mention a few. But inspite of all these achievements, the conspicuous absence of women in the public domain remains as paradox of the Kerala mode of development.

The economic marginalization of women in the development process has drawn considerable attention during recent years. The incidence of unemployment among females in the state is higher than that among males by five times in rural areas and three times in urban areas. The marginalization of women in the economic process and lack of control over resources have been major impediments in improving the status of women.

Kudumbasree

Kudumbasree was initiated by the left front political party, under the people's decentralization plan. This program aimed to organize women at the local level with the goal of eliminating absolute poverty in the state. *Kudumbasree* means "Prosperity of the family" and the mission of the programms is to reach families through women, and to reach communities through families. The programme began in 1996 in Urban areas, and then became active in the rural areas.

Kudumbasree has a three-tiered hierarchal system of organization. At the lower level are the neighbourhood groups (NHG) equivalent to the SHG. These groups are the federated at the ward level into Area development societies (ADS). The highest level is the community development society (CDS). The CDS is presided by an elected member of the ADS, and includes the Panchayat Presidents.

ECONOMIC IMPACT OF SELF-HELP GROUPS

Women have tremendous energies to start their own enterprises given the right opportunities. They have developed abundant self-confidence and self-esteem through self-help group movement not only to overcome economic poverty but also social and gender issues which can be tackled effectively through this process.

The micro-financing of women through self-help groups has helped the groups to achieve a measure of economic and social empowerment. It has developed a sense of leadership, organizational skill, management of various activities of a business, right from acquiring finance, identifying raw material, market and sustainable diversification and modernization.

THE CONCEPT OF SELF-HELP GROUPS

The theory of underdevelopment views poverty as a product of vicious circle of low per capita income, low savings and consequently low capital formation and productivity and so on. In rural areas it arises mainly from unemployment, underemployment and low earnings. Poverty reduction requires active involvement of the government, together with substantial non-governmental effort, to tackle it on two fronts simultaneously i.e., production and distribution and redistribution. Development of social infrastructure like education, skill and training is crucial to enable rural people to be gainfully employed, besides paying special emphasis on the provision of Basic Minimum Services (BMS). Poverty alleviation programmes came to be adopted only from the Fifth five year plans, as one of the principal objectives of economic planning. (Mishra and Puri, 2000).

Self-Help Groups are usually informal groups whose members have a common perception of need and importance towards collective action. These groups promote savings among members and use the pooled resources to meet the emergent needs of their members, including the consumption needs. The number of members in SHGs is normally ranged from 10 to 20. It is expected that, within the group, there should be true democratic culture in which all the members must participate actively in the decision making process by taking part in the debate rather one should say discussion. Though the cohesiveness among the members would be increased due to homogeneity of the groups in terms of education, occupation, income distribution, sex composition, but in the long term, stability of SHGs depends on their members loyalty to it and the adequacy of SHGs to meet the growing needs of the members.

Indian Initiative

The first effort was taken by NABARD in 1986-87 when it supported and funded an action research project on "Saving and Credit Management of Self-Help Groups" of Mysore Resettlement and Development Agency (MYRADA). Then NABARD launched a pilot project to provide micro-credit by linking SHGs with bank in 1991-92. During the project period, some NGOs like Association of Sarva Seva Farms (ASSEFA), People's Rural Education Movement (PREM), Professional Assistance for Development Action (PRADAN) and Community Development Society (CDS) have done excellent work in promotion of SHGs and mobilization of thrift and disbursal of credit. In 1999, Reserve Bank of India had set up a Micro-Credit Cell to make it easier to micro-credit providers to pursue institutional development process. Therefore, Micro-credit system had been considered as an important instrument to provide credit for self-employment and other financial and business services, including savings and technical assistance, to very poor persons. This is the concept of economic empowerment of the poor people through formation and nurturing of self-help groups (SHGs).

Women, who constitute slightly less than 50 per cent of the total population are generally under-employed due to their limited command over resources and regulatory institutions. Particularly, rural women face greater than their urban counterparts with no source of livelihood other than agriculture. Hence, the Government has been adopting various programmes for poverty alleviation of poor women in the country. The introduction of DWCRA was one such scheme. However, its several shortcomings leading to its failure, paved way for the introduction of self-help groups scheme, a sub-programme under Swarnajayanthi Gram Swarozgar Yojana. (SGSY).

The Swarnajayanthi Gram Swarozgar Yojana launched on 01-04-1999, aims to bring the assisted families (*Swarozgaris*) above the poverty line by ensuring appreciable sustained level of income over a period of time. The objective is to be achieved by inter alia Organizing the rural poor into Self-Help Groups through the process of Social mobilization, training, and capacity-building and provision of income generating assets. The SHG approach helps the poor to build their self-confidence through community action. This process would ultimately lead to the strengthening and socio-economic empowerment of the rural poor as well as improving their collective bargaining power.

Self-Help Groups go through various stages of evolution

- v Group formation (formation, development and strengthening of the groups to evolve into self-managed people's organisation at grassroots level): In our society, members are linked by various common bonds like community, blood relation, place of origin, activity, economic status, etc. The facilitators must identify these like minded natural groups which are commonly called 'Affinity Groups'. Identification of such Affinity Group is critical for the progress and success of the Self-Help Group. This would require staying with the people for some period to facilitate proper understanding and establish rapport with them. Therefore, while forming Groups, facilitators must recognise the natural bonds and affiliations existing within the society.
- v Group Stabilization through thrift and credit activity amongst the members and building their Group Corpus. The group takes up internal loaning to the members from their Group Corpus. The groups should save regularly and begin to lend to members. This provides the members with opportunities to acquire the skills to prioritize scarce resources, to assess the strength of each member, to time the loans and schedule of repayments and fix interest rates. The group institutionalizes the need to introduce sanctions for deviant behaviour, which could include delay in repayments, arriving late or absenting from meetings etc.

v Micro finance, the Group Corpus is supplemented with Revolving Fund sanctioned as cash credit limit by the Banks or the group could also have access to credit under the Self-Help Group-Bank Linkage Programme of NABARD.

v Micro enterprise development, Group takes up Economic Activity, of their choice for income generation. This phase would include Entrepreneurship Development as well as Skill Development Training of the members of the Group to enable them to successfully implement the chosen activity. All the Groups, particularly Groups formed with members who are skill less, asset less, destitute and living under object poverty might not graduate to the stage of Micro enterprise with in the time frame indicated in the Guidelines. Such groups may continue to remain in the Micro-Finance stage for a longer period of time and may require intensive training and capacity building inputs to enable them to reach higher levels of income generation.

Self-help Group Model

The Self-help Group Model was presented in Fig.1.1. The Self-help Groups go through various stages of group formation. Initially a bench mark survey is undertaken and problems are identified followed by other stages-conscientization, selection of groups, identifying roles of members.

The next stage is group action. At this stage, the members of the self-help groups will be given training related to technologies/production units and are linked with financial institutions like banks, credit unions etc. The other stage is facilitation which includes the change-agent intervention and implementation of corrective measures and the final stage is evaluation.

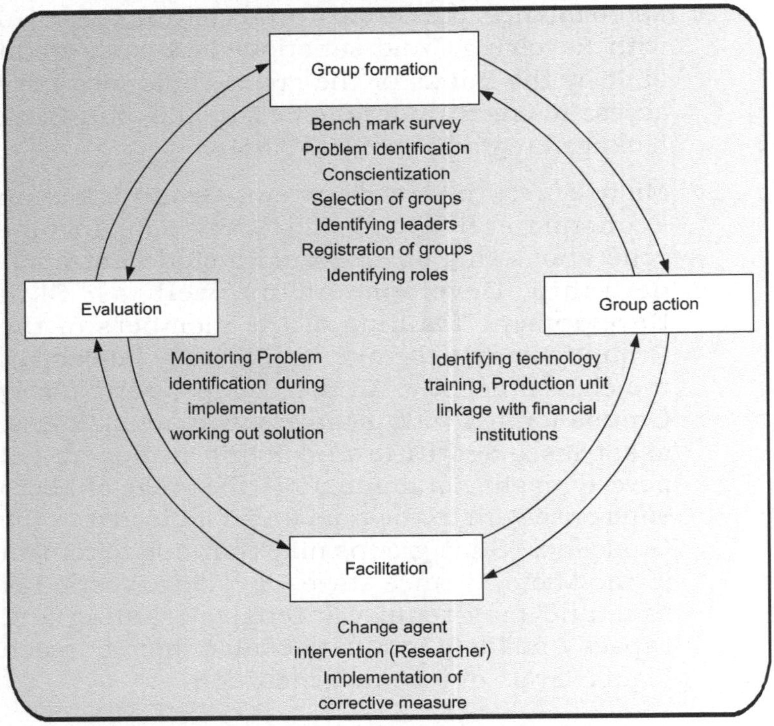

Fig.1.1: Self-help Group Model

In this stage, problems identified during implementation of the scheme will be monitored and workable solutions will be identified and implemented. If problem arises in the course of any of these stages, it may be corrected adopting corrective measures.

The reverse arrow in Fig.1.1 indicates that after group formation, monitoring and evaluation can be undertaken at each stage while selecting the groups, identifying leaders, registration of groups etc. As a part of general awareness/conscientization programme, these meetings emphasize the importance of groups, group formation and their importance in starting income generating activities. The members are made aware of the possibilities of income generating vocations and also about the credit facilities given by various financial institutions in starting such enterprise.

The strength of a group and its sustainability depends on the facilitation that has gone behind the formation of the groups. The group dynamics in fact reflects the kind of facilitation the group has undergone. Training is a critical input in the effective implementation of self-help groups. The members of the group consist of rural women, who come forward voluntarily, who have enough leisure time and are prepared to take up such enterprise. They are exposed to Entrepreneurship Development Programme as well. From this perspective the SHGs function in different stages.

Formation of Self-help Groups

The SHG is group of rural poor who have volunteered to organise themselves into a group for eradication of poverty of the members. They agree to save regularly and convert their savings into a Common Fund known as the 'Group corpus'. The members of the group agree to use this common fund and such other funds that they may receive as a group through a common management.

The group formation will keep in view the following broad guidelines:

i) Under the SGSY, generally a self-help group may consist of 10 to 20 persons. However, in difficult areas like deserts, hills and areas with scattered and sparse population and in case of minor irrigation and disabled persons, this number may be from 5-20. The difficult areas have to be identified by the State Level SGSY Committee and the above relaxation in membership will be permitted only in such areas.

ii) Generally all members of the group should belong to families below the poverty line. However, if necessary, a maximum of 20% and in exceptional cases, where essentially required, upto a maximum of 30% of the members in a group may be taken from families marginally above the poverty line living contiguously with BPL families and if they are acceptable to the BPL members of the group. This will help the families of occupational groups such as agricultural labourers, marginal farmers and artisans marginally above the poverty line, or who may have been excluded from the BPL list to become members of the self-help group. However, the APL members will not be eligible for the subsidy under the scheme. The group shall not consist of more than one member from the same family. A person should not be a member of more than one group. The BPL families must actively participate in the management and decision making which should not ordinarily be entirely in the hands of APL families. Further, APL members of the Self-Help Group shall not become office bearers (Group Leader, Assistant Group Leader or Treasurer) of the Group.

iii) The group should devise a code of conduct (Group management norms) to bind itself. This should be in the form of regular meetings (weekly or fortnightly), functioning in a democratic manner, allowing free exchange of views, participation by the members in the decision making process.

iv) The group should be able to draw up an agenda for each meeting and take up discussions as per the agenda.

v) The members should build their corpus through regular savings. The group should be able to collect the minimum voluntary saving amount from all the members regularly in the group meetings. The savings so collected will be the group corpus fund.

vi) The group corpus fund should be used to advance loans to the members. The group should develop financial management norms covering the loan sanction procedure, repayment schedule and interest rates.

vii) The members in the group meetings should take all the loaning decisions through participatory decision making process.

viii) The group should be able to prioritise the loan applications, fix repayment schedules, fix appropriate rate of interest for the loans advanced and closely monitor the repayment of the loan instalments from the loanee.

ix) The group should operate a group account preferably in their service area bank branch, so as to deposit the balance amounts left with the groups after disbursing loans to its members.

x) The group should maintain simple basic records such as Minutes book, Attendance register, Loan ledger, General ledger, Cash book, Bank passbook and individual passbooks.

Fifty per cent of the groups formed in each block should be exclusively for the women. In the case of disabled persons, the groups formed should ideally be disability-specific wherever possible. However, in case sufficient number of people for formation of disability-specific groups are not available, a group may comprise of persons with diverse disabilities or a group may comprise of both disabled and non-disabled persons below the poverty line.

By and large, the SHG will be an informal group. However, the groups can also register themselves under the Societies Registration Act, the State Cooperative Act or as a partnership firm. The SHGs can be further strengthened and stabilised by federating them at, say village or cluster of villages or block or District level depending upon the number of Self-Help Groups and their spatial distribution. The DRDAs may facilitate in planning of network of SHGs by federating them at appropriate level, once SHGs have reached the stage of maturity and have stabilsed. This would facilitate regular interaction, pooling of surplus with the groups, exchange of experiences including flow of information from DRDAs and other departments, bulk access to Credit from various Micro-Finance Institutions and help them to plan for desired backward and forward linkages including marketing of their products.

Social mobilisation and community organisation is a process oriented approach as different from target oriented approach. The group formation should not be driven by any targets but lend itself to a 'process approach'. The members of the SHGs should fully internalise the concept of self-help.

A large number of DWCRA groups have been formed and, assisted by DRDAs in the past. Likewise, there are a number of Self-help Groups formed by NABARD, other Banks, Rashtriya Mahila Kosh (RMK), Non-Government Organisations (NGOs), Women and Child Development Department under the Swa-Shakti and Swayamsidha etc. The DRDAs should put in concerted efforts to strengthen and consolidate these groups as some level of synergy already exists and then take steps to form new groups. Further, there is a need to develop data base on the Self-Help Groups formed and existing under various programmes in the district. The DRDAs may act as nodal agency for developing the data base, which should include Self-help Groups formed under all the

Fig.1.2: Administrative Structure of Self-Help Groups (State Level)

Administrative structure of Self-help groups state level agency			
Official Members	State level	Ministry of Rural Development Member/Secretary Joint Secretary Department of Rural Development and Ministry of Panchayatraj State level co-ordination committee	Non–Official Members
Official Members	District Level	Chairman Member/Secretary District level development agency for each District District Collector/Chairman Zilla Parishad Chairman (Vice-Chairman)	Non-Official Members
Official Members	Mandal Level	Member of Governing body Project Director (DRDA) Asst. Project Director (DWCRA)	Non-Official Members
Official Members	Village Level	Mandal Level organization Village level organization self help group leader	Non-Official Members

schemes. This would ensure convergence of various schemes as well as better planning for training and other requirements of SHGs.

The administrative structure of SHGs functioning at the State level encompasses the Ministry of Rural Development at the top and village level organizations at the bottom.

On the above basis, a large number of SHGs have been formed in both Andhra Pradesh and Kerala. The SHGs in India function on the lines of the above structure. However while some SHGs were highly successful in attaining the objective of improving the quality of life and empowering of women, the other groups failed to do so. Keeping this in view, the present research study focuses on the factors contributing to the success of SHGs.

JUSTIFICATION OF THE STUDY

Micro-credit programme through self-help groups is different from poverty alleviation programmes. It targets the rural and urban households below the poverty line and assures the poor women of employment and income. Micro-credit savings helps the women to come out of the clutches of the money-lenders. Further, savings can also be ploughed back into the common fund. Micro credit through self-help groups helps the poor women to build their skills and capacities and provide access to finances without any collateral and empowers them not only economically, but also socially.

In India, even today in certain regions and states majority of the women are plagued by illiteracy, poverty and lack of basic amenities in addition to the major responsibility of maintaining the family. This necessitated the effort to identify and take up various income generating activities to supplement the family's income which resulted in the formation of a large number of self-help groups in India. As such India has become one of the countries where SHGs and micro enterprise play an effective role in women's development.

Self-help Group in short, is a sustainable organizational setup which disburses micro credit to the poor women and encourages them to enter into entrepreneurial activities. Women lead self-help groups in many parts of our country have achieved success in bringing them to the mainstream of decision making. Self-help Groups serve as a source of inspiration and a viable alternative for achieving the objective of socio-economic development for women by involving them in all development programmes.

In Andhra Pradesh, there are about 6.5 lakh of SHGs functioning in the State formed by DRDA under the Indirakranthi Padam (IKP) programme. All the districts in Andhra Pradesh are covered by SHG bank linkage programme and Chittoor is one of the leading districts among them. The SHGs are also popularly called IKP groups. The study district has a record number of 50,000 SHGs, which figure significantly in a big way in eradicating poverty and empowering women. Similarly the state of Kerala also has made significant strides in the field of micro finance. The success of Kudumbasree and the wide publicity of SHG strategy have attracted several other agencies. Formal agencies like District Collectorate, Primary Agricultural Credit Societies, Department of Industries, Development of Agriculture and various other government agencies are how actively promoting SHGs in Kerala for the effective utilization of their funds.

The role of NABARD in the growth of SHGs in Kerala is worth mentioning. Kerala remains the third largest in the country next only to Karnataka and Andhra Pradesh in the matter of the number of linked groups and accounted for 13 per cent of the total linked groups in India in 1999 (Kerala Status focus paper, NABARD 2000). The number of self-help groups increased from 352 in 1994-95 to 2434 in 1999-2000, recording a growth of around seven times over a period of five years. The highest number of groups was in Alappuzha district (996) and the amount of bank loan distributed was also the highest in the district (Rs.131.09 lakh).

In our country, during the last five decades efforts have been made to improve the status of women by various strategies and through development programmes. The neglect of women in the development process and the immediate need for appropriate attention on women to enable to attain requisition position has been emphasized. The states of Andhra Pradesh and Kerala witness gigantic strides in terms of women empowerment through micro credit. However all SHGs are not equally successful. Therefore, research on factors which are figuring in the success of SHGs would facilitate the unsuccessful SHGs in their economic ventures. Research studies penetrating into these aspects are always essential to understand the process of SHG movement in a much better way for realizing the potential and benefits of Self-Help Group movement. Keeping this in view the present study was taken up.

SEQUENCE OF PRESENTATION

The thesis opens with the "Introductory chapter" and is followed by a brief discussion on empowerment of women through SHGs, conceptualization of empowerment, the information on SHGs, in India, and in Andhra Pradesh and Kerala was specifically presented in Chapter 1. "Review of literature was presented in detail in the Chapter 2. Chapter 3 gives the statement of problem, objectives and hypotheses. Methodology comprising of sampling, variables and their empirical measurements and the statistical methods used in the study was presented in Chapter 4. Chapter 5 deals with results and discussion. This has been divided into five sections. Section I deals with the socio-demographic and psychological characteristics of the SHG respondents. Section II describes the economic empowerment of Self-help groups. Section III deals with the findings about the components of empowerment. Section IV deals with effect of age and education on socio-psychological variables and components of empowerment, section V is devoted to the findings of the group variables. Summary and Conclusions were presented in Chapter 6, preceding Bibliography.

CHAPTER 2

REVIEW OF LITERATURE

A thorough review of literature is of paramount importance to any research endeavour. It helps to acquire a broad general background in the given field. A review of research studies already done in the area will be helpful in giving direction to further research. Research studies focusing attention on self-help groups and the different aspects of the development have been identified and presented with a view to get better insight of the research problem.

Most of the studies pertaining to SHGs are evaluative in nature, undertaken by agencies administering or funding the programmes. Such studies tend to focus mostly upon the quantitative dimensions of different types of self-help groups. Some studies have examined the economic aspects of the groups functioning while some others discuss the psychological aspects, in particular the "group dynamics". Certain other studies link the groups functioning to the ultimate objectives of rights and empowerment.

SHGs - A REVIEW OF PROGRESS

Micro-finance and women empowerment is a subject that has received growing research attention in recent years. Several organizations have promoted SHGs taking up the philosophy and approach of successful experiments of extending credit to poor women. Since the early 1980s, a large number of studies have examined the various dimensions of micro-finance programmes and women empowerment. Several international organizations such as Action-Aid, UK, CGAP (Consultative Group to Assist the Poorest), and Overseas Development Authority have conducted case studies and organized work shops in various countries. The workshops had looked mainly into the experiences of different countries and the impact of the micro finance programme in a cross-cultural perspective. Other sources of information include published and unpublished materials including materials from the Micro-credit summit (February 1997 and 2001) and action research programmes of IRMA, NIRD and CIRDAP Digest.

Though new to the informal sector debate, micro-enterprise promotion has evolved from poverty alleviation activities from the early 1960s. The proponents of micro-enterprise development approach are action oriented. They aim to empower groups and communities through business assistance and development of organizational skills and capacity. They promote, fund and carry out programmes that address the needs of the poor (Rakowski, 1994).

Choudhary (1996) in her study stressed the need for shaping women's empowering strategies to make them effective and result oriented. She pointed out that money earned by poor women is more likely to be spent on the basic needs of life than that by men and that this realization would bring women as the focus of development efforts. She also examined the advantage of organizing women groups there by creating a new sense of dignity and confidence to tackle their problems with a sense of solidarity and to work together for the cause of economic independence.

An article (Gramin Vikas, 1995) highlights the role of an innovative saving/credit programme called *Podupulakshmi* that had been successfully launched and carried out in the Nellore district of Andhra Pradesh. *Podupulakshmi* is based on a very simple principle of saving a rupee per day/per member. The aspirations of women for economic prosperity went up and they started climbing up the social ladder through the programme. The other factor for the success was timely intervention of the government machinery. The careful identification of key government functionaries also led to the success of the programme.

The South Malabar Gramin Bank (1998) conducted a "Monitoring Study on SHGs" to examine the progress of the scheme since its implementation in 1995-96 in Malappuram and Kozhikode districts. About 60 per cent of the bank-linkaged groups were rated as excellent. In a few groups, group dynamics decreased after the credit-linking. The study suggests that in 20 per cent of the groups, the organizational set-up should undergo change by replacing the existing members. It identified several weaknesses in the CDS groups such as lack of monitoring, lack of interest among co-ordinators due to non-receipt of allowance which they had been formerly receiving and static performance of groups.

An impact study conducted in seven wards with 2003 risk families in Alappuzha by the Department of Statistics, University of Kerala, revealed that families with less than two meals per day had gone down from 57 per cent in 1993 to 44.50 per cent in 1996, families with one or more illiterates fell from 26.5 per cent to 17.8 per cent and families with persons addicted to alcohol declined from 32.5 per cent to 22.10 per cent.

Studies on Concept of SHGs

NABARD (1995) defined SHG as a homogenous group of rural poor voluntarily formed to save whatever amount they can conveniently save out of their earnings and mutually agree to contribute to a common fund from which to lent to members for productive and emergent credit needs.

Singh (1995) conceptualized SHG as an informal association of individuals which come together voluntarily for the promotion of economic and social objectives.

A SHG is a homogenous group of not more than twenty-five individuals who have come together for greater economic and financial strength through mutual help (Anon, 1996).

Dwaraki *et al.* (1996) described a self-help group as an unregistered body of people, preferably the disadvantaged who willingly contribute an agreed sum of money which would be lent at a price for a short period as fixed by the group itself.

Krishnamoorthy (1996) defined SHG as an organization formed by people for pooling their resources to help each other.

Roul (1996) defined SHG as an institutional framework for individuals or households who have agreed to cooperate on a continuing basis to pursue one or more objectives.

Karmakuar (1998) defined SHG as an informal group of people where members pool their savings and re-lend within the group on rotational basis.

Shylendra (1998) defined SHGs are small informal associations created for the purpose of enabling members to reap economic benefit out of mutual help, solidarity and joint responsibility. The group-based approach not only enables the poor to accumulate capital by way of small savings but also helps them to get access to formal credit facilities.

Thomas (1998) defined SHG as a homogenous group of rural poor voluntarily formed to save small amounts out of their earnings which is convenient to all members and agreed upon by all to form a common fund corpus for the group to lend its members for meeting their production and emergent needs.

Studies Related to DWCRA

Rao (1995) conducted a study on "DWCRA – A means of women's empowerment", the present study endeavours to examine the functioning of DWCRA group at Bommaganipalli Village of Brahmasamudram mandal in Anantapur district of Andhra Pradesh. The selection of the DWCRA group was based on purposive sampling method. An unstructured interview schedule was administered to get the information from the members. The articulation skills and the achievements of the group space for the success of their empowerment. There is a greater scope to increase the production capacity of unit and further improve the marketing network through the involvement of governmental and non-governmental agencies which serve as one of the strong means to empower women.

Prasad (1995) conducted a study on "Development of women and children in rural areas: successful case studies". DWCRA is being implemented in 354 districts all over the country as a sub-scheme of IRDP. The objective of the programme is to raise the income level of women of poor households and enable them to become organized participants in social development and economic self reliance. Besides providing financial support for income generating activities, it also aims at increasing women's access to other welfare service. With this objective the present study was undertaken in Gurgaon district of Haryana. Some of the common factors for the success of the group are homogeneity, effective leadership, repayment procedures, systematic planning, quality control and marketing, support of officials are the key factors for the effective management of the programme.

Sitalakshmi *et al.* (1995) conducted a study on "dissemination of health messages to the beneficiaries of DWCRA programme. The sample selected was 100 women of DWCRA. The findings of the study were related to socio-economic conditions of the beneficiaries and dissemination of health message, to the beneficiaries and it helps the target groups in bringing spectacular changes in their awareness, attitude and involvement in health programmes.

Yadagiri (1996) conducted a study on "Rural poor and a challenging task of DWCRA: A study of women in A.P". The area selected was Nedunoor Village in Rangareddy district. DWCRA programme seeks to provide opportunities of Self-employment on a sustained basis. The women has also become socially aware of the need to educate the girl child and prevent social evils such as liquor consumption and child marriage. One women group organizer said that we have now realized that both boys and girls are the same, our daughters could also become collectors if they are educated. DWCRA members said it resulted in better quality of life because of access to literacy and health services. There is also betterment in nutritional status of families.

Rao (1997) conducted a study on DWCRA-an appraisal using indepth personal interview and through several visits. Findings reveals economic activities were mostly individual or family based and there was no substantial meeting ground to held the group together.

Rajakutty (1997) conducted a study on development of women and children in rural areas (DWCRA) in Tamil Nadu and Andaman Islands. The study's quick focus was on the Administrative arrangement and efficiency of IRDP implementation, taken up by National Institute of Rural Development. The author had an opportunity to took critically into implementation of DWCRA. Though a well-conceived scheme, its implementation has suffered and weakened its objectives. Assistance to women groups has been found to be relatively more productive and repayment performance was also better.

Thejaswini and Veerabhadraiah (1997) conducted a study on "Knowledge assessment of rural women on DWCRA and their problems" in Mysore district in Southern Karnataka. The study reveals that the women were encouraged in rural areas to participate in this programme so that they gain more knowledge about different trades and become self employed.

Yerramraju and Firdousi (1997) Conducted a study on women's Development: Issues, concerns and approaches" the study was conducted in three districts of Prakasam, Adilabad and Cuddapah districts of Andhra Pradesh, it brings out the patterns of group formation, group dynamics impact on the economic development and social cohesion among the women members and on employment generation. It highlights the need for disassociating the scheme from IRDP and for allowing it to blossom as self-help group programme capable of generating income and employment on its own plank.

Rao (1998) conducted a study on "DWCRA group of Pallipadu shows the way" Pallipadu village of Konikasia mandal is about 34 Km from Khammam town. The group had various options to go in, like pickle/papad making, handicrafts, readymade garments, wet grinding and leasing of land for cultivation. The group opted to go for leasing of land for cultivation. They were provided with bankloans for purchase of tractor, water used for agricultural activities. There is improvement in clothing, sanitation and children's education.

Prasad (1998) conducted a study on "DWCRA: Synthetic gem cutting units – some lessons to learn". This study was taken up in Periyar district with the sample size of 60 women from four units. The main objective of DWCRA is to provide income generating skill and activities to poor women by improving their social and economic status.

Sundaram and Singh (1998) conducted a study on "Assessment of DWCRA programme on modalities of operation". The study was conducted in Girwa Panchayat Samithi of Udaipur district with the sample of 58 beneficiaries of DWCRA groups. Major findings of the study were there was a change in the socio economic status, and in lifestyles before and after joining DWCRA group.

Nefa and Someshwar (1998) conducted a study on "DWCRA: A hope of light for women's development in rural areas". The study was conducted in Anantapur district, the sample consists of 117 beneficiaries covering 26 DWCRA groups. Majority of them belong to SC and backward communities. The age group of respondents were identified on the basis of availability of raw materials and skills, marketing facilities & individual choice. There are benefits like employment creation, income generation and health education, sanitation and improved conditions.

Manimekalai (1999) conducted a study on "Rural women beneficiaries of DWCRA scheme". The area selected for the study was Pudukottai in Tamilndau district. Large people of this district depend only on agriculture for their survival. The sample of 20 DWCRA group each consisting 20 members was selected randomly. 50 per cent of them were illiterates DWCRA women are considered significant in decision making at home, the overall health status of DWCRA women has improved.

Chatterjee (1999) conducted a study on "DWCRA groups in the Garo Hills", Meghalaya. The area selected for the study were Balasrigition the village of Samanda block and Damchiring the village of Samanda block. This study has revealed that DWCRA has contributed substantially for economic upliftment of the poor people, moreover it has helped them to work more unitedly with vigor and vitality.

Suneetha (2007) conducted a study on "Is DWCRA programme empowering the rural women" and inferred that there is significant growth in the employment generation of sample beneficiaries in Kodumoor mandal after the implementation of DWCRA.

Studies on SHGs and Micro-credit

Medha (2001) made a study similar to that of Sebastian, but Medha also covered the SHGs promoted by government agencies also in Maharashtra state. The title of the study was "Mobilising women SHGs through government and non-government organisations." which attempted to focus that how various governmental and non-governmental organisations stepped forward to empower women through Self-help Groups (SHGs). Total 160 SHGs were selected from three taluks viz., Bhor, Velha and Haveli of Maharashtra.

The study identified two major obstacles in the development of SHGs, i.e., enterprise training and marketing. Various government and non-government organisations were helping these women groups to become sustainable and viable. Pune Zilla Parishad had established Savior Centre for marketing, products made by SHGs and also given training to the manufacture of chalk, brooms, paper bags etc., For the first time in Pune district, a market at the taluka level was being set up which would cater to the various requirements of the taluka. SHGs, managed by the

Jijamata Research Centre of Gyantrabodhini at Shivapur, undertake various business activities. The centre provides enterprise training to the members of the SHGs and products manufactured by them had a market in California, USA. There were 20 members who contribute Rs.25 per month and deposit the amount in the Central Bank, Shikrapur by Shree Lakshmi Group at Jregan. This group has taken loan from Canara Bank, Waghole Branch for goat rearing on which they had to pay 13 per cent interest. SHG was formed by the NGO, Gramin Mahila Va Balak Vikas Mandal (GMVBM) funded by the Bank of Maharashtra. All the members were much more economically stable, active and successful today. The Bank of Maharashtra had taken the initiative for marketing the items like papad, chilly and turmeric powders etc. Study concluded from the above four case studies that the SHG movement holds the key to sustainable banking with the poor. The good performance in loan repayment had motivated banks to facilitate the formation of SHGs. Study suggested that the field staff should be well equipped in nurturing the development of the SHGs and should not succumb to pressure and hurry to meet the targets to attract subsidy.

Shishirkala *et al.*, (2001) made an interesting study on tribal women headed dairy enterprise. The study was conducted in Ranchi district of Jharkhand State and title of the study was "Economic Viability of Tribal Women Headed Dairy Enterprise: A case study."

The study was conducted with broad objectives of estimating the fixed and variable costs of different dairy units and to calculate the cost-benefit ratio of different dairy units to know the economic viability of tribal women headed dairy enterprises. Study found that the fixed cost accounted for 22.49 per cent of the total cost. Variable costs accounted for more than three fourth of the total costs. Out of this the cost of feed and fodder was found to be maximum. As part of the study it was observed that the bigger entrepreneurs were spending the least amount for producing one litre milk as compared to the entrepreneurs who had less than six cows. It shows that investment in dairy enterprise was economically viable and suitable for women particularly the tribal women in Bihar and Jharkhand States. Study concluded that the average net return of dairy enterprise was Rs.6,362 per month. The study further emphasized that with the active cooperation from NGOs and Government agencies the tribal women can prosper further in this regard.

Titus and Sebastian (2001) made a study on impact of micro-credit programmes operated by NGOs on rural women and the title of the study was "Impact of micro-credit programme of NGOs on Rural Women".

The study reviewed the micro-credit programmes of three NGOs Federations namely Gram Vidiyal and Sangamam operating in central Tamil Nadu. Objectives of the study were (1) to study the models emerging in the implementation of micro-credit programme by NGOs in the Tiruchirapalli district, (2) to find out the outreach of the programme; (3) to examine whether the programmes covered the people for whom it was intended; (4) to evaluate the micro-credit programme by measuring its impact on the participants; (5) to study the operational viability of the programme; and (6) to offer suggestions to improve the effectiveness of the programme.

The study revealed that the outreach of the micro-credit programmes showed an increasing trend in width and depth over the five years. Majority of the beneficiaries had taken the loans for productive purpose. Each of the programmes reviewed, covered about 300 villages and had a membership of about 1000. The programmes focused on rural women and at least a half of them belonged to scheduled caste. Study showed that NGOs had succeeded to a very large extent in reaching out to the poor through the micro-credit programmes. The impact of the programmes showed that more than 60 per cent of the respondents reported a monthly increase in income above Rs.300 arising of income generating activities. 81 per cent of the respondents had participated in the programmes for three years or more. Majority of respondents i.e., 87 per cent attended almost all the meetings without fail in a year. The members showed good understanding of the issues immediately concerning them at the group level. They were aware of issues such as dowry, voting rights, family planning. The study concluded that the micro-credit programmes have contributed to the growth of women entrepreneurs in the non-farm sector in a significant way and succeeded in contributing to the women's economic betterment which would lead to taking up of the micro enterprises by them in the long run. Recovery rate was very close to the cent per cent mark in all five years in all NGOs. The annual joining rate range from 20 to 45 per cent, which shows that the programme was continuously expanding over the years. Study also suggested to strengthen the programmes.

Basu *et al.* (2002) made a similar study on empowerment of women and the title of the study was "Empowerment of women in the context of development: some issues and suggestions".

The study examines the impact of development programmes on women in terms of their access and control over resources along with their standard of living so also the necessity for empowerment in the context of development and group awareness both at the individual as well as group community level. Data were collected from 13 villages from three districts of West Bengal through interview method. The study observed that the concept of post-natal checkup was almost absent among the women of the village, particularly among the low income and less educated section of the population. The uni-dimensional development programme for improving maternal healthcare/ status for pregnant and lactating women had so far failed to achieve the desired results. Khasjalashi, a village of Panchala block, Howrah district, has been selected for the study of DWCRA group in operation. Two DWCRA groups had been organized from the two hamlets of the village by a locally based NGO. Promoting self-employment scheme through DWCRA scheme was good enough for helping the socially deprived and poor women. The promotion of Jeri embroidery works by forming DWCRA group enlarges the scope for women of both religious groups of the area to become economically self-sufficient. About 55 SHGs groups had managed to get loans from their own group within a period 1996-2000. Promotion of sustainable eco-friendly livelihood systems through animal husbandry, encouraging small entrepreneurship, promotion of savings habit and provision of credits for SHG members through different financial institutions created good effect on village women. Even non-member women showed interest in savings. DWCRA Project had made a significant contribution by providing financial assistance for self employment of the village women. Study concludes that the Women empowerment had been considered as a tool for community development which helps the women to accept a particular model of empowerment through income and awareness generation programmes designed by academicians/ politicians/government/administrators development activities/donor agencies and NGOs.

Institute of Social and Economic Change made a study on "Micro-finance, Poverty Alleviation and Empowerment of Women: A study of two NGOs from Andhra Pradesh and Karnataka." The study attempts to find out the economic and social benefits of the micro-finance programmes on members of micro-finance groups. Primary data were collected from the project area of two NGOs in Karnataka and Andhra Pradesh, namely, Gram Vikas and Sanghmitra Service Society respectively. These two project areas are located in Kolar and Krishna districts in Karnataka and Andhra Pradesh respectively. Data were collected through survey method, focus group discussions and semi structured discussion. Total 106 members households in six micro-finance group were collected for this study purpose.

The study showed that the micro-finance programmes do provide economic benefits to the people for whom the programmes were initiated. These economic benefits were mostly continued to availability of savings and credit facility, access to credit for consumption and production and use of credit for undertaking income generation activities. It found that economic benefits which more pronounced in the project area of Gram Vikas suggests that there were factors other than the microfinance at work here. There are availability of larger funds for income generation mostly due to NABARD's Bank-SHG linkage programme and donor funds, and the existence of infrastructure (developed dairying activity in terms of well spread out marketing outlets). The study concluded that the micro-finance programmes do provide access to credit for the poor, enable them to undertake income generation programmes and contribute to higher recovery rates. The responsibilities such as development of economic infrastructure and providing additional funds to micro finance groups must be undertaken by the government as the micro-finance programmes can not alone alleviate the poverty. Thus, ISEC's study further proved that micro-finance through SHG network has been the best bet for forging a coordinated effort for development of women.

Gupta, (2002) made a study on "Formation and functioning of SHGs in Hoshangabad district of Madhya Pradesh" with the Objective to examine the working of, Self-Help Groups in the State of Madhya Pradesh, in general, and in village Dandi Junkar, in particular. Dandi Junkar in Kesla block of Hoshangabad district was selected for the study. The village is having eight SHGs and the district has the largest number of SHGs in the state. Data were collected from the branches of the State Bank of India, District Co-operative Bank, Regional Rural Bank at Suktawa and Co-operative Society in the same village, which catered to the needs of SHGs of the village. Discussions were also held with the members of SHGs to get the information.

The study observed that the SHGs held meetings regularly. All the members regularly save some amount of money. SHG members work for a minimum period of six months as a savings and credit group. The SHG maintained records, meetings, member wise savings, common fund, fund creation/maintenance, loans given from common fund and recoveries etc., If none of the members of SHG group is literate, the son or daughter of any member writes the accounts and minutes of the meeting. The bank branch opens a savings bank account, in the name of the SHG, for which the Reserve Bank of India has issued necessary permission to the banks. Study found that in Madhya Pradesh till 31st March, 2000 a total umber of 2272 SHGs were linked with branches of banks. These SHGs were given loans to the tune of Rs.4.10 crores and refinanced of Rs.2.77 crores. In Hoshanngabad district 216 SHGs had saving bank accounts with the branches of different banks. Regional Rural bank Sukatwa, had a total number of 168 SHGs District Central Co-Operative Bank, Kesla had saving book accounts of 35 SHGs State Bank of India, Kesla and Punjab National Bank, Tawanagar had 10 and 3 savings bank accounts respectively. For the year 2000-2001 it was estimated that 250 additional SHGs would be formed. Study also observed that the formation of SHGs in such a large number in Hoshangabad district could be due to untiring and dedicated work of NGOs namely PRADAN, NCHSE and BAIF. They initiated the work through Mahila Samithies in tribal villages. It is suggested that both the elements of targets and achievements for the government servants and bank subsidy would make the programme not only mechanical but also dilute the co-operative spirit among SHG members and hence the same could be avoided.

Jyothy (2002) made a study on SHGs in Tamil Nadu titled "Self-help Groups under the Women's Development programmes in Tamil Nadu: Achievements, Bottlenecks and Recommendations" and found that women development depends upon capacity building, awareness and health, education, environment, legal rights, functional literacy and numeracy, communication skills, leadership skills for self and mutual help. Economic empowerment of women is also vital and the study profiles self-help groups of Mahalir Thittam (Womens' Development Programme) in Tamil Nadu and there are over 26,000 groups as on March 2000 in the State. The data on self-help groups reveal high degree of motivation and determination to succeed. On the basis of indicators, the growth of self-help groups and its members, percentage of SC and ST members, growth of savings and internal lending are discussed. The economic activities of SHG groups include production and marketing of *agarbathis*, candles and soaps, readymade garments, pickles, *papads* and other items. The self-help groups are also enable women to perform various self-sustained activities, such as proper functioning of the ration shops, maintain vigil to prevent brewing of illicit-liquor, help the aged, deserted and widows, grow vegetables in their kitchen gardens and maintaining group unity and transcend barriers of caste, creed and religion. External credit linkages are essential to foster the financial sustainability of the SHGs. The study recommends removal of bias against SHGs by the bank officials, and each bank should have a special cell to assess the activities of SHGs and clusters should also be favorably disposed towards them to sustain the programme.

Kafmakar *et al.* (2002) critically examined the role of women in SHG formation and also the issue of cooperation in a detailed manner through their study entitled "Role of women in the SHG: An emerging possibility to co-operation at grass-root". The study examined the performance of the Self- Help Groups and co-operative societies in Midnapore district of West Bengal. Altogether 20 self help groups emerged in the Sankrail area of the Midnapore district. functioning well in the area. Experiments of SHGs are each SHG comprises of 10-20 members. Women meet together for the SHG meetings and at the same time they gain some knowledge on different problems of the village and their development also. Groups rotate the money to the needy members for various purposes at a specified interest rate. As the repayment is cent per cent and the recycling is very fast, the savings amount increases faster. The saving habit paves the way for the empowerment of women and builds up confidence in them that they could stand on their own feet. Self-Help Groups are linked with the banks for the external credit under the projects of rural development. Banks provide financial assistance for various entrepreneurial activities such as setting up of petty shops, vegetables shops, charcoal making units and dairying etc. Self-Help Groups enhance the equality of status of women as participant decision makers and beneficiaries in the democratic, economic, social and cultural spheres of life. They encourage women to take active part in the social economic progress. The SHGs bring out the supremacy of women in moulding the community in right perspective and explore the initiative of women in taking up entrepreneurial ventures. So far 14 SHGs have sanctioned loan amounting Rs.24,850 and in 10 SHGs Rs.7,700 had been repaid within one year period. Rate of the overall rate of recovery was more than 50 per cent. Recoveries among all the 18 SHGs varied between 43.29 per cent and 7.35 per cent respectively. In cases of SHGs loan repayment has been 33.33 per cent to 35.29 per cent. SHGs had inculcated a great confidence in the minds of rural women to succeed in their day to day life.

Kaur *et al.* (2002) made a study in Tamil Nadu on Women Entrepreneurs in rural areas. The title of the study was "Rural Women Entrepreneurs: A Study in Rural Tamil Nadu." The objectives of the study were to identify the entrepreneurial talents of rural women and to find out the willingness of women entrepreneurs to learn new skills or improve their existing skills and their entrepreneurial interests. About 107 rural women were selected from three blocks of Dindigal district of Tamil Nadu. Data were collected through structured interview schedule.

The study observed that out of 107 respondents, only 19.6 per cent were skilled and the percentage of semi-skilled women was much higher with 79.4 per cent. About 50 per cent of the respondents were ready to learn or improve their talents. The number of women willing to improve their talents was more in backward block. About 49% of the rural women in the backward block were willing to start their own enterprise whereas in the developing block, only 25 per cent of them were willing to set up such enterprises. As regards the reasons for not starting their own enterprises, 4.5 per cent of women expressed lack of interest, 10.5 per cent of women did not have the motivation and energy, 46.2 per cent respondents were already occupied in other economic activities, 28.3 per cent expressed lack of confidence and awareness and 10.5 per cent reported not having money required to start an enterprise. Prevailing conventional customs and way of living, norms of modesty, male dependence and male dominance, illiteracy etc. were the other factors which had negative impact on the rural women in starting their own enterprises. It is suggested that technical and financial assistance may be provided to rural women and efforts should be made to educate them and improve their entrepreneurial management and marketing skills.

Thus, the study elucidates the micro-level conditions which are hindering the promotion of women enterprises in rural Tamil Nadu. The spark within appears to be the prime factor in forging women empowerment as considerable of rural women in this context expressed certain motivational and awareness factors as prime reasons behind starting their own enterprises.

Reddy (2002) in his study on "Empowering Women Through Self-Help Groups and Micro-Credit: The Case of NIRD Action Research Projects" made an attempt on how Self-Help Groups promoted among women as part of Action Research leads to women empowerment. The study describes that thrift and credit was strategic entry point for the action research intervention in Ranga Reddy district of Andhra Pradesh.

The study concluded that organisation of self-help groups and development of their institutional and managerial capacity is an imperative element in the empowerment process of women. The formal financial institutions such as banks DRDA had come forward to extend loans for income-generating activities for SHG members. Women interacted with external agencies and professionals with confidence, which was an evidence of improved social skills and approachability. They were able to be particular about their needs and seek help from various schemes of development.

Thus, the observations of the study confirm the process that concept of Self-Help Group approach would certainly help women to overcome their difficulties and follow successful path of self-development. The study confirms that participation in Self-Help Groups would certainly lead to development of certain social skills besides providing economic independence.

ORG-MARG Research Limited, Hyderabad made a elaborate study on self-help groups operating in Andhra Pradesh in a study entitled "Strengthening of Self-Help Groups in Andhra Pradesh : Swot Analysis of the Groups Surveyed in Andhra Pradesh." The study made the following general observations on SHGs formed in Andhra Pradesh:

Strengths

1. Groups are homogenous and cohesive; Group membership based on Income, Caste and Neighbourhood.
2. Member composition: SC = 22 % ST = 4 % BC = 49% Others = 25%; High percentage of women in fertility group; Mean age of members 35 years
3. Flexibility in group management: The Group decides independently on Interest Rate, Prioritizing Loans, Social Pressure
4. Purpose of Group Formation: Savings = 56% Future Security = 25%, Self-help = 25%, Loans = 8%
5. Group exercises social pressure to inculcate thrift and regularity in attendance: Action taken against chronic absentees 24%; Non-conformity leads to expulsion from group

6. Regularity in savings (saving from necessity and not always from surplus) Defaulters in the last three months 8%
7. Purpose of saving: Future security = 68% Self-help = 16% Avail loan = 15%
8. Creditworthiness assessed: On the basis of Income and occupation = 49% Past Repayment Record = 30%; Property owned = 27% Faith in member = 17%
9. Issues discussed in Group meetings: Health/ Sanitation = 5% Janmabhoomi = 29% Village problems = 22%; Household problems/needs = 14% Family Planning = 12%
10. Gradual shift from consumption loans to productive loans: Purpose of Loans, Productive Loans = 82%, Consumption Loans = 18%;
11. Dependence on money lenders among members is declining: Members would have gone to moneylenders there had been no SHG-61%; Members would not have started the activity there had been no SHG-7.5%
12. Loan recovery rates are high.

However, the study also pointed out certain weaknesses in the SHG movement in Andhra Pradesh. These were:

Weaknesses

1. Participation of Widows and Destitute: Widows/ Destitute in the group—9%
2. Groups over dependence on the leader: The leader manages all activities regarding Accounts, loans and attendance, etc., Members involvement in mobilization of savings—4%.

3. Development of leadership among other members is lacking Leadership Rotation in 13 Groups
4. High illiteracy among women resulting in poor book- keeping and maintaining records, illiterate group members—75%.

Patil (2002) conducted a study on rural development programmes and their impact on women beneficiaries of Dharwad district of Karnataka during 1999-2000. Selection of villages was done by random sampling technique and 120-beneficiaries from eight villages were selected purposively who had taken self-employment as a venture. The information about various developmental programmes being implemented in the Dharwad district was collected from the Block Development Office and Zilla Parishad. Out of those different schemes TRYSEM and DWCRA programmes were selected, because these programmes helped maximum number of women beneficiaries to start self-employment. The independent variables selected for the study were, age, education, occupation, caste, marital status, type of family, family sizes, type of house, land holding, annual family income, social participation and mass media participation. Knowledge were the dependent variable. The data were collected by personal interview method by using pre-tested schedule.

The data revealed that education, social participation and mass media participation had positive and significant relationship with the level of knowledge of beneficiaries. However, no relationship existed between knowledge level and remaining independent variables like age, family type, family size, land holding, annual family income and extension contact. An educated women would be in a better position to collect, interpret, utilize and related information in day to day life. Though their participation in social institution was very low, their indirect participation either as member or office bearer might have contributed to gain knowledge. Mass media are important sources of information. Women who were exposed to mass media gained better knowledge.

The study reinforces the belief that the inner-self of women should be strengthened first to make them on par with men in rural societies. Education has nevertheless played vital role in the study under reference. Further, women need to be exposed to mass awareness campaign to gear themselves for developing receptivity to participate in development activities.

In a similar study of Rangi *et al.* (2002) titled "Economic Empowerment of Rural Women through Self-Help Groups : A Case Study of Fatehgarh Sahib district (Punjab)" which was conducted with the objectives (1) to study the socio-economic profile of members of the self-help groups (SHGs), (2) to examine the credit availed by the members of the SHGs and (3) to study the impact of SHGs on income generation for its members. The Fatehgarh Sahib district was randomly selected. Out of five development blocks two blocks namely, Khamano and Khera were randomly selected. From Khamano 26 SHGs and 39 SHGs from Khera blocks were selected. Twenty-five members each were randomly selected from various SHGs in both the blocks. Information was collected through personal interview method. Secondary information was collected through published sources.

Study revealed that the majority of the respondents of the SHGs were in the young age group and educated, though, the level of education was not very high. Two-third of them had their own land but majority of them belonged to the small and marginal farmers families. Study found that about 18, 62 and 20 per cent of the respondents of three districts became member of the SHGs in the years 1998, 99 and 2000 respectively. Before 1998, no SHG was set up in the Fatehgarh Sahib district. All the respondents saved a sum of Rs.100 per month with their respective SHGs. Forty-four per cent of the respondents borrowed from the internal sources of the SHGs during the year 2000-01 and 62 per cent had taken loans from the banks with the help of SHGs. The amount of loans taken from the banks was high as compared to the internal borrowing firm, the SHGs but the rate of interest was high in the later category. The internal and externalloans to the members of the SHGs have benefited them for their economic empowerment. The additional income generated with the help of SHGs have provided them big normal support and will to bring new changes in the rural economy of the State as well as of the country in future.

Rizwana (2002) examined the economic empowerment of women through her study on "Economic empowerment of women through women development corporations: A Study of Maharastra Women Development Corporation." The study made a detailed examination of process of women empowerment by examining the working of Mahila Arthik Vikas Mahamandal limited, (MA VIM), the activities undertaken by it and the benefits derived by the women's beneficiaries.

The study was carried out in Amravati district of Maharashtra. To facilitate implementation of the programmes, activities for the development of the women in Maharashtra, MA VIM, was established. Under its various schemes activities were introduced such as kerosene scheme, offering dealership to sell Kerosene, setting up of canteens for selling eatables, provision of accommodation for working women by setting up working women's hostel, and assistance in sale of stationery articles. Also assistance was extended by way of supply of nutritious food (snacks) to primary school students. Apart from MA VIM, Maharashtra Rural Credit Programme (MRCP) assisted by International

Fund for Agricultural Development was also implemented in the State which has helped the population by way of grant of loans for various rural development activities. In spite, the various schemes implemented under MA VIM and MRCP, it was noticed that due to rapid change in the requirements and expectations of the rural population the affectivity of the scheme was not satisfactory and there were shortcomings in their implementations. Further, MA VIM has implemented Maharashtra Emergency Earthquake Rehabilitation Programme to help the Latur earth quake victims which resulted in the diversion of the resources of MA VIM.

Roy Burman *et al.* (2002) in their study on "A glimpse into self-help in tribal areas", analysed the programme of Self-help Groups in tribal areas in India. In most cases SHGs are formed through active involvement of nongovernmental organisations (NGOs) or vo1untary organisations. It is observed that the element of self-help has been taken up at the expense of the state structures-weakening the sovereignty of the state. The main importance of SHGs is to link up the grass roots development processes and financial transactions to the international monetary order. According to NABARD data (1999-2000) SHGs availing credit has increased from 3,941 in 1997 to 81,780 in 2000. The total number of SHGs linked to banks stand at 1,14,755 in March, 2000. Eighty-five per cent of them are women groups. The number of financial institutions, extending credit to the SHGs has increased from 120 in 1997 to 266 in 2000. The SHGs are operating in 362 districts of 24 States and Union Territories. The number of NGOs dealing with SHGs has increased from 220 in 1997 to 718 in 200p. The recovery rate in some select villages of different States was 37.88 from non-SHG members and 92.30 per cent from SHG beneficiaries. The poorest are generally not members of any SHG and in some villages, they are not even aware of the efforts, made by NGO/banks in forming groups in their village. This feature is common in the tribal areas of all the states covered in the study. It is found that nearly 30 per cent of the SHGs covered under the study evolved from pre-existing groups (PEG) in rural areas. In the tribal areas covered, the SHGs are successful more among the powerful and the richer groups. It is concluded that the system has only one point agenda-earning income. SHGs may often appear to be self-reliant, but in reality they are not. It should be realised SHG formation and the associated activities reflect a posture of populism and there are inherent dangers in it. The authentic self-help activities in the tribal communities are possibly the ones, which can withstand the onslaughts of neoliberalism.

Sarada Devi and Rayalu (2002), in their study on factors functioning in women empowerment in urban areas conducted in Hyderabad, identifies various aspects related to the empowerment of women and assesses the level of differences between working and non-working women in the perception of women's empowerment. Seventy-five working and 75 non-working women were selected randomly from the twin cities of Hyderabad and Secunderabad of Andhra Pradesh. Data were collected though interview schedules. Study showed that working women perceived more problems due to more power in the family than non-working Women. Non-working women faced problems due to powerlessness when compared to working women. Non-working Women had more aspirations related to power as they were deprived of required power status in the family. Both working and non-working women felt that their personal freedom and self-interest were their first priority in power persuasion. The power ratio was better for the working women than non-working women and more number of non-working women used different strategies to get power. More number of non-working women perceived discomfort in performing their daily roles and experienced more restrictions on them as compared to the working women. Lack of freedom to spend money, inability to pursue self-interests, loss of personal mobility and authority of spouses on personal affairs were the problems experienced by the non-working women.

In the past Puyalvannan (2003) made a study on SHGs in Tamil Nadu. The study Micro-credit Innovations : A study based on "Micro Credit, Women empowerment and living of SHGs with co-operative banks in two districts in Tamil Nadu", was conducted in Trichy and Pudukkottai district of Tamil Nadu. The study revealed that, SHGs has formed by fifteen approved NGOs in the Pudukkottai and Trichy districts. The members have granted loans for varieties of purposes, both productive and unproductive. Results have shown that women are credit worthy and responsible users of credit. Recovery is monitored by the group members and they are discussed regularly in the group and group meetings. The recovery is reported to be 90 per cent in the Pudukkottai district. Social impact of SHGs operation in the area show that the women members have achieved political empowerment by winning elections in panchayat boards. SHGs have established effective networking with other government organisations, NGOs etc. Many SHGs were given micro entrepreneurship training and they have equipped the members to do varieties of activities.

Further, women members attended literacy camps, conducted meetings of the groups regularly, discussed freely problems with officials and go to the extent of meeting district collector frequently with written complaints about required developments in their respective areas. Panchayat works are undertaken by SHGs with the efforts of group members. Area development and members development are visibly seen through SHG and linkage activities. At the initial stages NGOs and women development corporation have dynamic role in forming SHGs in Tricy district. Finally, the study observes that poor women are credit worthy and responsible user of credit, facility and systemic rule minded.

The study, thus supports the view that as far as microcredit is concerned women are at most advantageous stage and if, at initial stages, women are loaded properly through awareness etc. they can cross all the hurdles and can take care of their own economic development.

Sudharani *et al.* (2003) conducted a study on SHGs and empowerment found that the participation in the self-help groups enriched the women in house managements, health and sanitation, leadership qualities and economically. The decision-making capacity of the SHG participants increased with the period of participation.

Rao and Sarojani (2005) conducted a study on "Tribal self-help groups – strengths and weaknesses" and revealed that majority of the sample have inclination and interest towards political participation and are well aware about banking system.

GROUP CHARACTERISTICS

Group interaction

Muller (1997) reported that social participation and training showed a positive correlation with group interaction in effective groups.

Sreedaya (2000) reported that planning, production and marketing aspect of vegetables were found to be positively and significantly correlated with group interaction.

Rama Rao and Kurmacharyulu (2002) found that the members joined in the group with the expectations of getting income, income generating activity has also been taken by the group with a spirit of group approach, the position improved after joining in the groups and holding regular group meetings and sustainable flow of additional income.

Group Cooperation

Goutam and Simha (1990) Opined that the problem of non-functioning of DWCRA groups in Himachal Pradesh was due to lack of cooperative zeal among members of the group.

Bardhan (1993) revealed that cooperation works better in small groups with similarity of needs, clear boundaries and shared norms and patterns of reciprocity.

Muller (1997) reported a positive and significant relationship between social and extension participation and group co-operation.

Sreedaya (2000) opined that cosmopoliteness and high social participation would influence behaviour as a result they show more cooperation with the members of the group.

Group leadership

Hari Kumar (1990) reported that the success of group forming programmes depends on effective farm leader.

Neog (1991) reported that prevalence of common felt needs among group members is the basic requisite of group forming success and it is significantly associated with dynamic leadership.

Seethalakshmi and Jyothimani (1994) reported that the leadership role played by the group organizer is of great importance in making DWCRA group active.

Sreedaya (2000) reported that the leadership of Kerala Horticulture development programme (KHDP) SHGs functions in a better way due to the concept of master farmers.

Need Satisfaction

Shaw (1993) reported that a self help group can be sustainable only if it serves purposes important to its members.

Muller (1997) found that training gives the members of the group more knowledge leading to achievement of group goals and hence increase need satisfaction.

Sreedaya (2000) reported that as the people are more experienced and more success oriented they are able to tackle their problems more wisely and try to satisfy their needs.

Team Spirit

Mukherjee (1997) reported that some people in community have individualistic approach and do not easily get involved in community efforts. Participatory group approach depends largely on collective activities, initiatives and efforts.

Sreedaya (2000) reported that members who do not had high perception about the group will try to maintain a cohesion within the group and develop team spirit.

Venkata Ravi (2004) conducted a study on role of NGOs in promotion of SHGs reported that the women find ways and means of additional income generation by taking up micro-enterprise at the village levels. The collective for gaining strength has indirectly increased the confidence of poor to take the income generating activities for augmenting their earning capacity.

Equity

Hay (1995) observed that equity means people enjoying equitable access to opportunities. Development without equity means a restriction of choices of many individuals in Society.

Fernandez (1998) reported that for the sustainability of self help groups the equity should be ensured.

Sreedaya (2000) found that to develop a sense of equity among members participation either as a member or as an office bearer is required.

Accountability

Surendran (2000) reported that there is high level of accountability in quasi governmental groups and non-governmental organizations.

Sreedaya (2000) reported a positive correlation between accountability and educational status and experience in vegetable cultivation.

Interdependence of members

Hussain (1992) reported that interdependence of group members is a very important characteristic affecting group cohesiveness.

Muller (1997) reported that if members feel that they can work independently they should be removed from the group and the members who are willing to work with interdependence alone need be retained as a member of the group.

Sreedaya (2000) observed that higher age, educational status and social participation might have created a better awareness among the members about their role in the group and they try to help each other for the prosperity of the group.

Transparency

O'Brien (1997) is of the opinion that governance involving participation and transparency were essential for sound development.

Cambesus (1998) observed that increasing transparency of government operation decreases the chances for corruption and enhances public accountability.

FAO (1999) observed that transparency has to built into management functions in farmers organizations no matter whether leadership is shared or not.

Sreedaya (2000) defined that transparency is one of the effective ways to ensure fair and equitable delivery of goods and services to the people.

SOCIO-DEMOGRAPHIC AND PSYCHOLOGICAL CHARACTERISTICS

Age

Jayalakshmi (1996) Stated that age has a non-significant relationship with the entrepreneurial behaviour of rural women.

Varma (2002) Stated that age is significant factor that can influence the attitude of farm women towards starting their own enterprises in agriculture and allied areas.

Education

Jayalakshmi (1996) found that education was positively and significantly related to the entrepreneurial behaviour of farm women.

Muller (1997) stated that in effective groups, the educational status of the respondent showed a positive correlation with group cooperation.

Extension Participation and Training

John (1991) found that more membership in groups itself had enhanced the extension participation of the members and he found that extension participation has positive and significant influence on adoption of pepper cultivation practices.

Muller (1997) reported a positive and significant relationship between extension participation and group decision making.

Thomas (1998) reported that training was positively and significantly related with farm women's role perception.

Social participation

Varma (2002) in a study on a multidimensional analysis of self employment among farm women revealed that Social participation had a positive and significant relationship with attitude towards self-employment.

Thomas (1998) observed that a positive and significant correlation exists between social participation and participation of farm women in watershed development programmes.

Te-so-riero (2006) conducted an evaluation study of women's self help groups (SHGs) in an area in South India. Groups were evaluated not in terms of their success in micro-credit schemes but in relation to their contribution to gender development. Evidence emerged that women perceived changes in their identity towards working collectively to influence for change at the village and panchayat levels. They engaged in community and social action programmes, both at the local level and by joining with issues beyond the local level.

Mass media contact

Porchezian (1991) found that mass media contact is not significantly related with entrepreneurial behaviour of farmers.

Lalitha and Nagarajan (2004) conducted a study on "Empowerment of rural women through self help groups" revealed that the dynamic functioning of SHGs in the villages has resulted in spread effect, increase in savings, repeated visits to panchayat union office demanding various amenities etc. Which the groups had availed certain benefits like street light, roads etc.

Achievement Motivation

Seema (1986) reported that no significant relationship between achievement motivation and participation in implementing decision by farm women.

Thomas (1998) found that achievement motivation had a non significant effort on extent of participation of women in watershed development programmes.

Sreedaya (2000) reported a positive and significant relationship between achievement motivation and need satisfaction of farmers.

Credit orientation

Nizamudeen (1996) observed that credit orientation behaviour of jasmine flower growers had prompted them towards successful adoption of the cultivation practices.

Sindhu (1997) reported that a non-significant relationship between credit orientation and conceptual skill of cut flower growers.

Sreedaya (2000) observed a positive and non-significant relationship between credit orientation and planning production and marketing aspects of vegetable farmers of KHDP and IVDP self help groups.

Economic Motivation

Shanthi (1996) reported that earning money to meet day to day requirements is the prime motive of women labourers in rice farming and hence economic motivation has emerged as the most contributing variable to managerial efficiency of these farm women.

Sivaprasad (1997) found that economic motivation is an important character that persuades people to adopt improved practices that are proven worthy.

Thomas (1998) reported that the more one is motivated by economic ends, the more he will try to adopt practices which are aimed at increasing sustainable returns.

Appa Rao (2002) reported that DWCRA has major impact in building self-confidence, economic development, social empowerment and development of skills.

AREA-BASED STUDIES ON SHGs IN INDIA

Cohesiveness of DWCRA Groups in West Bengal

Ghosh (1995) has made a case study of DWCRA in Birbhum district of West Bengal. The district was brought in the map of DWCRA in 1992-93. In the year, 18 women groups were formed in two blocks of the district. Among these groups only 10 groups were selected for the study by the author on the basis of their performance in respect of undertaking income generating activities. Sociometric score of each group member of these 10 groups is calculated to find out 'Stars' and 'isolates' of each group. A star is defined as a member who obtained a score significantly lower than the mean score. Pattern of choices like reciprocated choice i.e., mutual choices, and the number of choices received by individuals are the indicators of group cohesiveness, 'Stars' and 'Isolates' in a functional group.

Next, correlation co-efficient between educational status and cohesiveness was calculated to find out whether it has any bearing. It was found to be 0.57, indicating a positive and more or less high relationship between educational status and group cohesiveness. Hence, for enhancing group cohesiveness it appears necessary that educational status of women members must be improved.

For finding the relationship between group cohesiveness and income and share of each group in total earnings of all groups is computed. It is clear from the study that until group cohesiveness is adequately built up, DWCRA groups cannot drive the full benefits of the programme.

Lessons from IRMA Project

Shailendra (1999) attempts to evaluate the performance of 8 women's self-help groups promoted in the village Bidaj by the Institute of Rural Management, Anand (IRMA) under an action research project called model village project. The SHGs were created to act as instruments of savings and development for the women. Though the SHGs could be created fairly easily, overall they failed in the first three years in their objective to enable members to realize the potential benefits. As a result, the SHGs failed to make any significant impact on the socio-economic life of the women members. On the basis identified for the failure of SHGs are: wrong approach followed in SHGs formation by the team, misconceptions about SHGs goals both among the team and the members of SHGs and lack of clarity about the concept of SHG particularly by the team leading to failure in ensuring conditions necessary for their successful functioning. A few lessons drawn from the project include; the need for creating SHGs based on clear assessment of the needs of different sections, taking care to avoid any major misunderstanding among members about the goals and purposes of SHGs: ensuring a clear understanding of the concept of SHG among team members involved in promoting SHGs and the need to enhance the relevance of SHGs to their members by enabling them to meet effectively their requirements, be it savings or credit or income generating activities.

Findings from MYRADA Experience

Puhazhendhi and Jayaraman (1999) have made an empirical study of the performance of informal groups promoted by Mysore Resettlement and Area Development Agency (MYRADA), an NGO based in Bangalore. They have chosen the Credit Management Groups (CMGs) promoted by MYRADA purposively for their study, keeping in view the fact that CMGs have enlarged the role of access to credit and entrepreneurship development. Primary data collected from 25 randomly selected CMGs framed the basis for the analysis. The groups were selected from two different project areas, viz. Chitradurga district in Karnataka and Periyar district in Tamil Nadu. For the purpose of quantifying the factors that influence women participation in different stages of group development, the groups were post stratified based on the age group functioning. Group in the age group up to 2 years were categorized as new groups, where as groups in 2-4 years and above four years were categorized as stabilizing and stabilized groups respectively. The extent of women participation in various activities of the group was assessed through comparing the pre-and post-group formation situations. Benchmark survey data available with NGO, along with the primary data collected from the members of the selected groups, have been used to quantify the impact of group formation on women participation and employment generation.

In terms of occupational pattern of the members, agricultural members constituted 70 per cent of the membership of the groups followed by non-farm activities (15%). Rural artisans constituted nine per cent of the group members while six per cent of them were marginal farmers cultivating mainly under rained conditions.

The rate of saving per member varied from Rs.840 in new groups to Rs.1,845 per annum in stabilized groups, the average being Rs.1,068. An analysis of the groups in different stages of development has revealed that the share of loan for non-productive purposes was significantly reduced from 76 per cent in new groups to 43 per cent in stabilized groups. Similarly, the loan for productive purpose increased from 24 per cent in new groups to 57 per cent in stabilized groups. Good repayment performance (more than 95 per cent of recovery) by the members of the groups and groups to banks were positive feature that confirm active participation of women in the common activities and the informal functioning.

The enterprise combination of women revealed that as a result of group formation, women were able to diversify their activities through undertaking non-farm and animal husbandry activities. Members taking up more then one activity increased from about 30 per cent during pre-group formation to about 53 per cent during post group formation situation. As a result, the average annual net income of the members was doubled.

SUMMING UP

The foregoing review of literature reveals that development is a complex phenomenon, with many forms and many causes. Yet, while human deprivation can take a number of forms, its essential features are remarkably similar across countries and locations. With this background the empirical investigation of the problem role of self-help groups in women's economic development was undertaken, as this process differs from the individual beneficiary oriented schemes experimented earlier. The next chapter deals with the statement of the problem, objectives, hypotheses and limitations of the study.

CHAPTER 3

STATEMENT OF THE PROBLEM, OBJECTIVES AND HYPOTHESES

Micro-credit programmes through self-help groups is different from other poverty alleviation programmes. It targets the rural and urban households below the poverty line and assures the poor women of employment and income. Micro-credit savings helps the women to come out of the clutches of the money lenders. Further, savings can also be ploughed back into the common fund. Micro-credit through self-help groups helps the poor women to build their skills and capacities and provide access to finances without any collateral and empowers them not only economically, but also socially.

In India, even today in certain regions and states, majority of the women are plagued by illiteracy, poverty and lack of basic amenities in addition to the major responsibility of maintaining the family. This necessitated the effort to identify and take up various income generating activities to supplement the family's income which resulted in the formation of a large number of self-help groups, in India. As such, India has become one of the countries where SHG and micro enterprise play an effective role in women's development.

NEED FOR THE STUDY

Poverty has remained the biggest challenge in India's development efforts to bring about a perceptible change in the quality of life of its teeming millions. India being a developing country, a vast section of its population suffers from malnutrition, unemployment and poor health care. This is particularly true in the case of the four main weaker sections of the society namely, women, children, scheduled caste and scheduled tribes.

In rural India, the high rate of illiteracy and low economic status of women, underline the need for increasing their earning power by providing the income generating assets. Provision of employment opportunities and income to rural women is one way to improve their nutrition, health, education and social status. In most of the developing countries, greater emphasis is laid on the need for development of rural women and their active involvement in the main stream of development. In our country, continuous efforts are being made by the Union and State governments to improve the status of rural women, especially those below the poverty line through different schemes of rural development.

Ever since independence a number of innovative schemes have been launched for the upliftment of women in our country. There has been a perceptible shift from viewing women as critical agents for socio-economic development. Now the emphasis has shifted from development to empowerment of rural women.

Women constitute one-half of the segment of pluralism in India. The 2001 census counted 495.7 million females against a total population of 1027.01 million, in which 207.8 million women live in the rural areas and 27 per cent of the rural women live below the poverty line. Enhancing women's economic productivity is an important strategy for improving the welfare of 60 million Indian households below the poverty line. Hence, the emphasis is laid on the empowerment of the rural women focusing on the following aspects. They are:

a) Direct involvement of women in programming and management.

b) Effective collaboration with community organizations.

c) Organizing and strengthening of women's self-help groups.

d) Sensitization and advocacy for gender just society.

e) Identifying women's needs and priorities while generating employment.

f) Organizing women in different groups to undertake certain productive activities to earn their livelihood, and to develop the rural community.

But women remain at the helm of affairs in the process of development. The rural and urban slum women play a major role in mobilizing and activating the rural development activities. One such important activity is self-help groups. As the programme is in implementation since 1986, it needs some empirical study to enable both women and the Government to set higher returns from the schemes. Therefore, it is indeed essential to examine the extent to which women are benefited through rise in per capita income through income generating activities.

In view of the growing importance attached to women's development in the process of Rural Development and by and large economic development of the country, the timely attempt is made which may be proved useful in the planning and framing of Rural Development Models which are similar to the activities of other developing countries such as Bangladesh. Framing a development model which is related to women would bring positive results. The necessary support services are to be provided both by government and society at large. Such support services for rural women are provided under SHG and DWCRA programmes which brings about women empowerment.

Women empowerment means the idea that gives women power over their economic, social and reproductive choices which will raise their status, promote development and reduce population growth. "Women empowerment can be viewed as a continuum of several interrelated and mutually reinforcing components".

- Awareness building about women's situation, discrimination, rights and opportunities as a set towards gender equality. Collective awareness building provides a sense of group identity and the power of working as a group.
- Capacity building and skills development, especially the ability to plan, making decision, organize, manage and carry out activities to deal with people and institutions in the world around them.
- Participation and greater control and decision making power in the home, community and society.
- Action to bring about greater equality between men and women.

Self-Help Groups in short, is a sustainable organizational set up which disburses micro-credit to the poor women and encourages them to enter into entrepreneurial activities. Women lead self-help groups in many parts of our country have achieved success in bringing them to the mainstream of decision making. Self-help groups serve as a source of inspiration and a viable alternative for achieving the objective of socio-economic development for women by involving them in all development programmes.

However, all self-help groups have not successfully contributed to the up-liftment of the poor women. Therefore, in order to find out what are the factors contributing to the success of self-help groups, the present research study was undertaken.

OBJECTIVES OF THE STUDY

In the parleys of social science research, it is quite essential to design the study comprehensively to address the basic issue of the study. Keeping this in view, care has been taken to understand the various important aspects of the study through selecting the objectives in the following manner:

The General Objective of the Study

- v To examine the self-help groups and its beneficiaries in Andhra Pradesh and Kerala and identify factors contributing to success and failures of the self-help groups.

The Specific Objectives of the Study

- v To study the socio-demographic profile of SHG women beneficiaries in the state of Andhra Pradesh and Kerala.
- v To assess the level of participation of self-help group women in decision making in family and community in the Andhra Pradesh and Kerala.

- To examine the impact of the programme on employment generation of self-help group women in Andhra Pradesh and Kerala.
- To assess the improvement in the economic status of women in Andhra Pradesh and Kerala before and after joining self-help groups.
- To compare and analyze the components of empowerment in the state of Andhra Pradesh and Kerala, and
- To analyze the group characteristics of self-help group women beneficiaries in Andhra Pradesh and Kerala.

HYPOTHESES

Based on the above objectives, the following hypotheses were formulated:

There is no significant difference in the socio-demographic and psychological characteristics of SHG women beneficiaries in Andhra Pradesh and Kerala.

- Differences in the levels of participation of SHG women of Andhra Pradesh and Kerala had no significant effect on the decision making capacity at family and community level.
- There is no significant improvement in the economic status of SHG women beneficiaries in Andhra Pradesh and Kerala after joining SHG programme.
- There is no significant variation in the components of empowerment of SHG women beneficiaries in Andhra Pradesh and Kerala and
- There is no significant difference in the group characteristics of SHG women beneficiaries in Andhra Pradesh and Kerala.

BRIEF DESCRIPTION OF THE VARIABLES

Independent variables

Age – The number of calendar years completed by the rural women at the time of interview.

Religion – The religion to which the rural women belongs.

Caste – The caste hierarchy of rural women, whether belongs to upper/backward/scheduled caste.

Family size – The specific number of members in the family living together.

Family structure – The single type (nuclear) family or joint family, extended family.

Occupation of the respondents – The position of the family which acts as a source of income in which she spends major part of her time and attention.

Educational status of the respondent – The levels of formal education attained by the respondent.

Educational status of the family – The level of formal education attained by the members of the family.

Family economic status – The position of the respondents family with reference to income from agriculture/job/business, houses owned, property owned and material possession.

Annual income – The total earning of the family from farm and other sources.

Landholding – The total land owned by the rural woman.

Social participation – The extent and nature of participation of rural woman in various activities of social organization.

Mass media contact – The extent to which a rural woman is exposed to different mass media communications such as radio, newspaper, television.

Cosmopoliteness – The degree to which a rural woman is oriented to her immediate outside social system.

Attitude towards self-employment – The degree of positive or negative feeling of rural woman towards self employment.

Credit orientation – The favourable and positive attitude of an individual rural woman towards obtaining credit from institutional sources for self employment.

Persuasiveness – The ability of a rural woman to influence by arguments, by reasons, by inducements or to with over other person to accept something to be true, credible essential, commendable or worthy.

Self-esteem – The respondents sense of personal adequacy or inadequacy and a sense of having achieved (or not achieved) need satisfaction in the past.

Group Variables

Group interaction: The tendency of members to mix freely with each other without inhibition.

Group leadership: The effectiveness of the leaders in changing the attitude of members to maintain the group stable and enhance the success of the group.

Transparency: The extent to which the working of the group are clear and known to the members of the group.

Need satisfaction: Achieving individual members necessitates by the group within a specified time.

Inter-personal trust: The extent to which members trust on each other for the successful functioning of the group.

Team spirit : The co-ordinated efforts, both physical and mental aspects of the members in order to achieve the best possible results derived by the group.

Equity : The group approach minimizes or removes the inequalities in the distribution of inputs, credit, resources and output among its members.

Accountability : The extent to which members are responsible and answerable for their action or achievement of objectives as decided upon.

Limitations of the Study

Circumstantial limitations may act as barriers and prove detrimental in case of many efforts aimed at achieving something. Similarly, this endeavour could not be relieved from the clutches of such limitations. Basically, the study was handicapped to the extent that it was a single venture, covering one *mandal* of Chittoor district of Andhra Pradesh and one *mandal* from Palakkad district of Kerala State. Irreversible and irrevocable time and intermittent pecuniary constraints were the next irrefutable limitations.

CHAPTER 4

METHODOLOGY

It was observed that the economic support or economic independence of women changes the status of women both in the family and society. From the literature reviewed so far it was clear that the income earned by women directly meets the family consumption, education and health needs. In the light of the above discussion the present study aims to examine the role of self-help groups in women's economic development. This chapter deals with the details of the research design used, the procedure followed in selection of sample, the strategies and tools adopted, collection of data, mode of scoring and the statistical procedures deployed to interpret the data.

RESEARCH DESIGN

Ex-post-facto research design was followed for the present study. This method is generally used to study varying influence of two identical factors.

According to Kerlinger (1964) *Ex-post-facto* research design is a systematic empirical enquiry in which the scientists do not have direct control of influencing independent variables because their manifestations have already occurred or because they are inherently not manupalable.

Inferences about relations among variables are made without direct interventions from concomitant variations of dependent and independent variables. In this research study, since the manifestations of the independent variables had already occurred and as there was no scope for the manipulations of any variable, ex-post- facto research design was adopted.

LOCALE OF THE STUDY

This study was conducted both in the States of Andhra Pradesh and Kerala. In Andhra Pradesh, the study was conducted in Chittoor district and in Kerala, the study was undertaken in Palakkad district. A sample of 200 SHG women from Andhra Pradesh and 200 SHG women from Kerala were selected for the study. Thus, the total sample comprises of 400 SHG women beneficiaries (see figure 4.1 to 4.3).

The study area was purposively selected for the following reasons.

- v The investigator belongs to Kerala and was settled in Andhra Pradesh.
- v Madanapalle and Ottapalam mandals are the two mandals where active and effective maximum number of self-help groups are functioning

The investigator was familiar with both Malayalam and Telugu languages and this facilitated quick data collection.

Salient Features of the Study Area

ANDHRA PRADESH

Andhra Pradesh is the fifth largest state in India both in area and population. It has an area of 2,75,045 sq. km, the population of the state is 7,62,10,007 with a growth rate of 13.86 during 1991-2001. The major

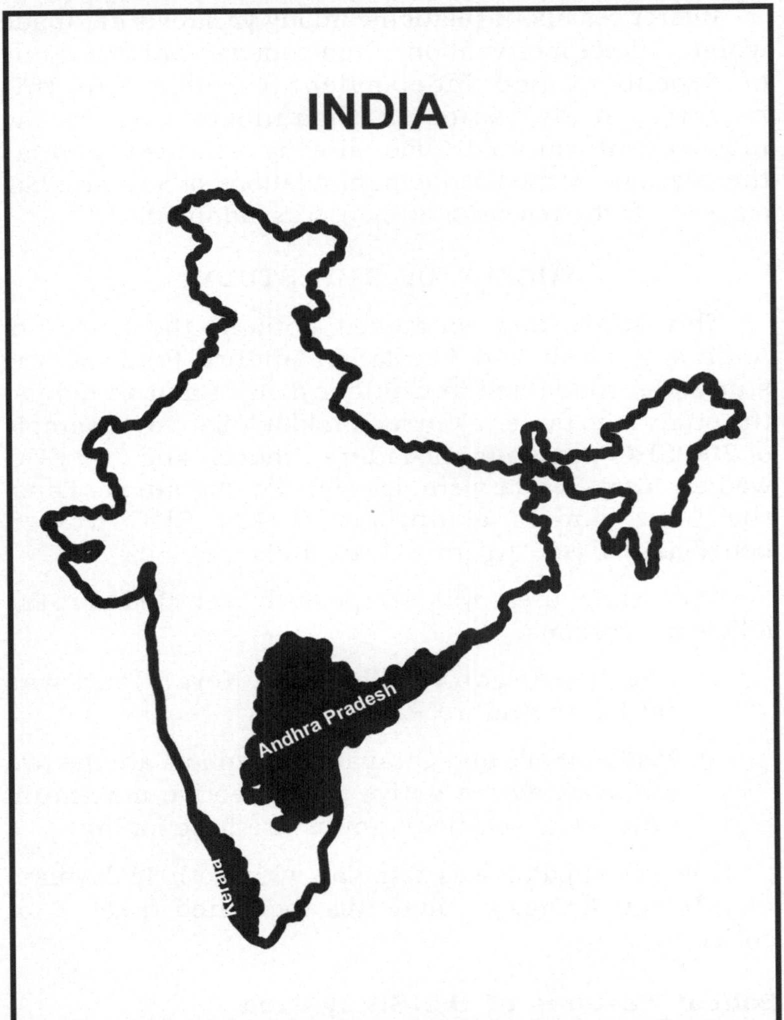

Fig. 4.1: India: Study Area

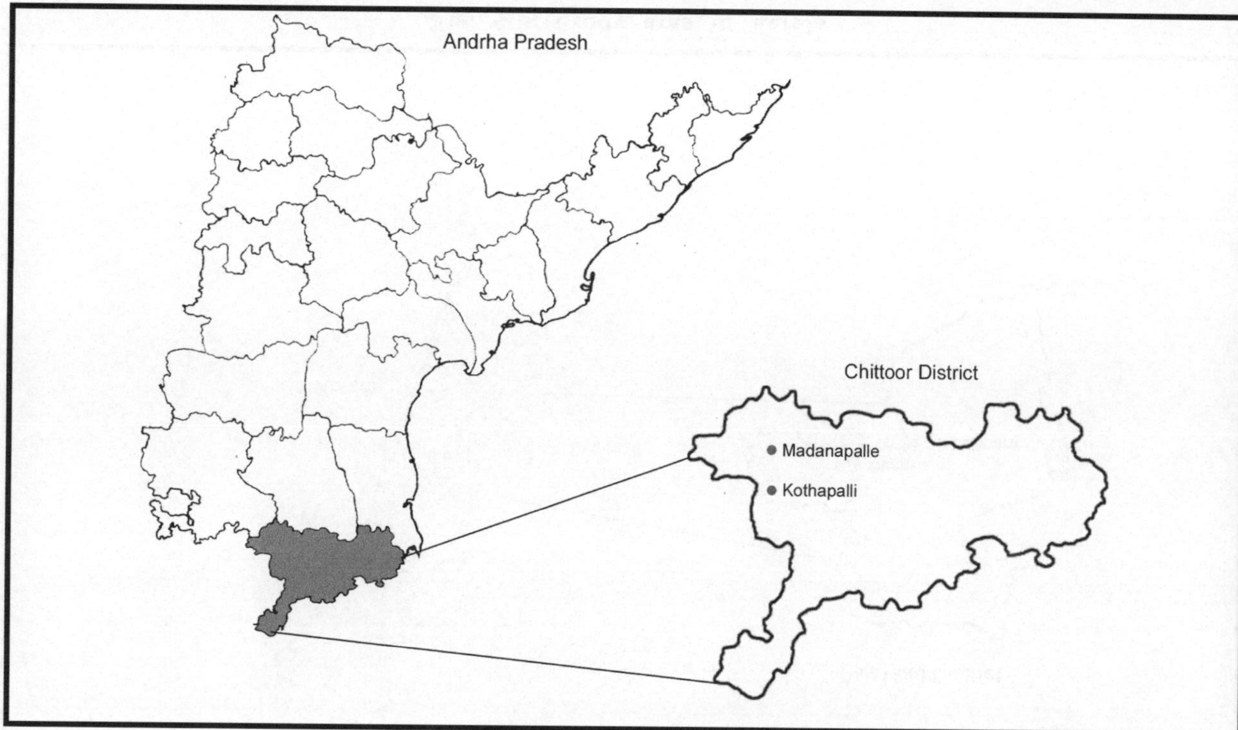

Fig. 4.2: Study area in Andhra Pradesh

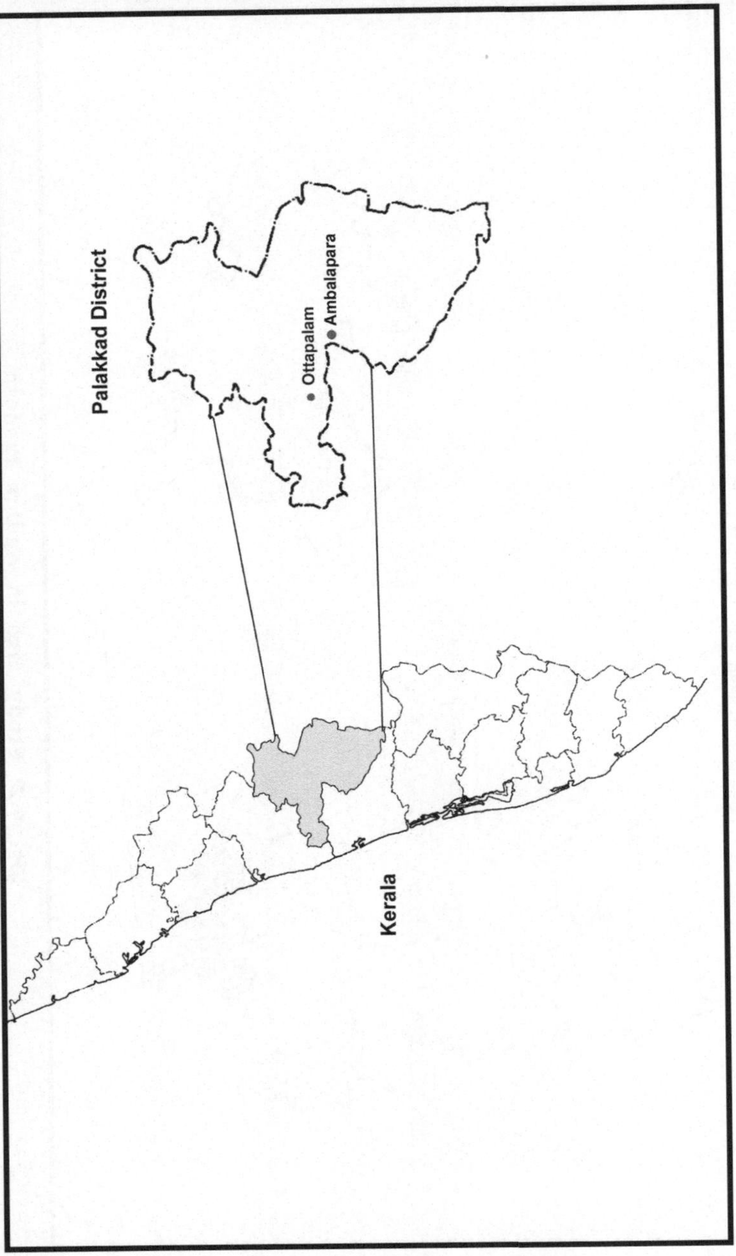

Fig. 4.3: Study area in Kerala

languages spoken in the state are Telugu and Urdu. The Government of Andhra Pradesh has declared Urdu as second language in 13 districts in view of a sizeable Muslim population. The density of the population is 275 per a sq.km. (Table 4.1). The urban population is around 27.08 per cent. The general literacy rate as per 2001 census is 61.11 per cent. The male literacy rate and the female literacy rates are 70.85 per cent and 51.17 per cent respectively. Andhra Pradesh still continues to be a rural based state having a rural population of 73.11 per cent and city population remained at 26.89 per cent. Nearly 69 per cent of the geographic area is being cultivated. Rice is the most important food crop while groundnut, sugarcane, cotton and tobacco are important commercial crops.

Table 4.1: Basic Information of Andhra Pradesh, 2001

Capital	Hyderabad
Language	Telugu
Land area	2,75,045 sq.km
Population, 2001	7,62,10,007
Population density	275 per sq.km
Literacy rate	61.11

The entire State is covered by 23 districts with three broad regions namely coastal region containing nine districts, Rayalseema region with four districts and Telangana region with ten districts. Ananthapur is the biggest district where as Hyderabad is the smallest.

Chittoor District: A Profile

Chittoor district is on the extreme South of Andhra Pradesh, between 12°37′ - 14°8′ north latitudes and 78°3′ - 79°55′ east longitudes. It is surrounded by Ananthapur and Cuddapah districts on the north, by Nellore and Chengai-Anna districts of Tamil Nadu on the east, by North Arcot Ambedkar and Dharmapuri district of Tamil Nadu on the South and by Kolar District of Karnataka on the west. The district is spread over 15152 sq. kms. As per 2001 census the population of Chittoor district is 37.35 lakhs. The male literacy rate is 77.62 per cent and female literacy rate is 55.78 per cent.

The various industries of Chittoor district generating employment for the people are sugar, ceramics, textile, railway wagon workshop, alcohol, moped, brass and copper. The popular handicrafts of the region are wooden crafts, Kalamkari and bell metal and stone crafts. The forests of the region help the nation to earn foreign currency by exporting teak and red sandal wood. The other by products of the forest are honey, tamarind, and many ayurvedic plants, which earn revenues for the State.

The district of Chittoor is well connected to the various places of the State by rail and road. The headquarters of Chittoor district is at Tirupati which is the nearest airport. The district receives electricity from the Thunga Bhadra Hydro Electric Project. Chittoor is a favorite destination for pilgrims, temples like Lord Venkateswara Temple, Srikalahasthi Temple, Tiruchanoor Temple etc. are the famous pilgrim centres. The major food crops grown in Chittoor district are paddy, jowar, sugarcane, bajra, ragi and groundnuts. An urban commercial crops, groundnut takes the first place followed by sugarcane. Mango is one of the important orchard crops in the district. The district comprises of three revenue divisions and 66 mandals. Madanapalle is one of the revenue mandals among these.

KERALA

Kerala is located on the South Western tip of India. One is first struck by the greenness of the State, full of coconut grooves, paddy fields, coffee plantations and forests. Kerala is home to 32 million people, whose livelihoods depend largely on agriculture. The density of the population is very high. Kerala has been declared fully literate and the State language is only spoken in Kerala. Malayalam newspapers are the most frequently read newspapers in the country. The most prevalent religion in Kerala is Hinduism, although there are significant population who practise Islam, Christianity and Jainism.

Table 4.2: Basic Information of Kerala, 2001

Capital	Thiruvananthapuram (Trivandrum)
Language	Malayalam
Land area	39,000 Sq. Km.
Population, 2001	31,838,619
Population density 2001	819 per Sq.Km.
Literacy rate	90.92%

Palakkad District: A Profile

Palakkad is one of the fourteen revenue districts of Kerala. The district, situated almost in the centre of the state, has no coastal line. Western ghats is perhaps the most influential factor for the unique characteristics of the district such as climate, commercial as well as cultural exchanges between the State and the rest of the country. Palakkad witnessed invasions of historical importance that have left indelible impressions of the history of Kerala. Bharathapuzha, the longest river in Kerala, originates from the highlands and flows through the entire district.

The district is one of the main granaries of Kerala and its economy primarily agriculture. Agriculture engages more than 65 per cent of the workers and 88.9 per cent of the district's population is rural in nature. The proximity and easy approach to Tamil Nadu have caused the admixture of Malayalam and Tamil Culture here. The total geographical area of the district is 4480 sq.km representing 11.53 per cent of the State's geographical area. As per 2001 census the population of the district is 26,17,072. The density of population is 584 per sq.km. The sex ratio is 1068 females per 1000 males. The district has achieved 84.31 per cent literacy in 2001 and the male literacy rate is 89.73 per cent and female literacy rate is 79.31 per cent. The district is divided into 13 community Development Blocks for the effective implementation of various development activities.

"Rice bowl of Kerala" is the synonym of Palakkad. The net cultivated area of the district is 284 lakh hectares i.e., 64 per cent of the geographical area. Paddy alone accounts for about 60 per cent. Coconut, groundnut, cotton, sugarcane, pepper, banana and cashew are some of the major cash crops raised.

Selection of Sample

The study was conducted in both the States of Andhra Pradesh and Kerala. In Andhra Pradesh, Madanapalle *mandal* of Chittoor district was selected. From Madanapalle *mandal*, Madanapalle urban Panchayat and Kothapalli rural Panchayats were selected because it consists of larger number of self-help group women beneficiaries. In Kerala, Ottapalam *mandal* of Palakkad district was selected. From Ottapalam *mandal*, Ottapalam urban Panchayat and Ambalapara rural Panchayats were selected purposively for the above study. The list of self-help groups from the selected villages and mandals was obtained from the records of mandal office, DRDA office, SJSRY and SGSY office and municipal corporation.

From the 523 SHGs, 100 SHG members from Madanapalle urban panchayat and 100 SHG members from Kothapalli rural Panchayat were selected randomly, thus the total sample comprises of 200 SHG members belonging to nineteen groups. Each SHG group consists of 10-15 members. Similarly, from Kerala, of the 720 groups 100 SHG members from Ottapalam urban Panchayat and 100 SHG members from Ambalapara rural Panchayat, belonging to 15 groups were selected purposefully. Each SHG group consists of 10-20 members. Thus, a total sample of 400 SHG respondents belonging to Andhra Pradesh and Kerala. Formed as the final sample for the present investigation. Detailed sample frame is given in Fig. 4.4.

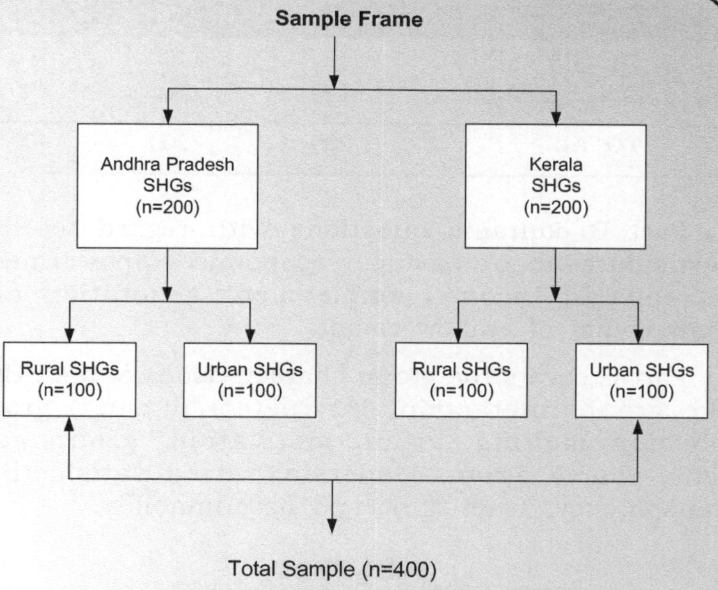

Fig. 4.4: Sample Frame of A.P. and Kerala

DEVELOPMENT OF INTERVIEW SCHEDULE

An Interview schedule was prepared carefully to collect the information from the respondents. The interview schedule consists of three parts. Part A covers the general information like age, religion, caste, education, marital status, annual income of the family, educational status of the family, land holding, family structure, family size etc. Apart from this, Part A also covers contact with the extension agency, social participation, mass-media contact, decision making in family and community, credit orientation, perception about SHGs, attitude towards self-employment, self-esteem and cosmopolite ness.

Table 4.3: Distribution of two categories of respondents in Andhra Pradesh and Kerala

Sl. No.	Types of SHGs	Andhra Pradesh	Kerala	Total
1.	DWCRA - SGSY	100	100	200
2.	DWCUA-SJSRY	100	100	200
	TOTAL	200	200	400

Part B contains questions with regard to SHG particulars about savings, economic empowerment, increase in income, employment generation and components of empowerment.

Part C covers the group characteristics of the SHGs like group interaction, interpersonal trust, group decision making, group motivation, group goal achievement, group leadership, need satisfaction, transparency, team sprit and accountability.

PRE-TEST

Pre-test was done on 50 SHG women beneficiaries belonging to five groups, other than study area of Andhra Pradesh and Kerala The investigator administered the interview schedule personally by visiting the SHG members. Results showed that there was no major difficulty in understanding the items but a few items had to be modified and a few had to be included. Final schedules were used to study the role of SHG members in economic development. The schedule thus prepared was translated both in Telugu and Malayalam languages for easy administration.

RELIABILITY OF THE INTERVIEW SCHEDULE

The co-efficient of reliability and validity of the interview schedule was established on a random sample of 50 SHG women. Test-retest method was used. The obtained correlation coefficient for the schedule was 0.783 which was significant at 0.01 level of probability.

Validity of the Interview Schedule

The interview schedule possess face validity, content validity and intrinsic validity as it has been established. The details of each of these are given below:

Face validity

The schedule was shown to 50 SHG women members who had no knowledge of empowerment, they felt that it measured the knowledge on economic empowerment and its components. Lindquist (1966) says "a test is face valid particularly if it looks valid to layman" and therefore the interview schedule has face validity.

Content Validity

Content validity indicates how adequate is the content of a test sampling the domain of which inferences are to be made. It is particularly important for research. To restore this type of validity to the test, an attempt was made to see that all the areas of economic empowerment were included. Under each component, an adequate number of sample items were included. The preparation of interview schedule was preceded by a thorough and systematic examination of all components of economic empowerment in books and journals. Experts were consulted. The interview schedule was reviewed in the light of the suggestions of the experts for content adequacy and accuracy. In view of these, it may be said that the interview schedule possess content validity.

Intrinsic Validity

The degree to which a test measures what it measures may be called its intrinsic validity. This definition can also be stated in terms of how well the obtained scores measure the tests true score component. The validity is indicated by the square root of the proportion of true variance, in other words, the square root of its words, the square root of its reliability. Another name for this statistic is the index of reliability. (Guilford, 1954). The intrinsic value of the test was

$$\sqrt{0.783} = 0.8848$$

which indicates that the schedule possess high intrinsic validity.

Table 4.4: Different Variables and their Measurements

Sl.No.	Variables	Empirical Measurement
1	**2**	**3**
1.	Independent Variables	
	(Socio-demographic Variables)	
	Age	Chronological age of the respondents
	Religion	
	Caste	
	Educational Status	Scale developed by Trivedi (1963)
	Marital Status	-do-
	Type of House	-do-
	Type of Family	-do-

1	2	3
	Land holding	-do-
	Occupation	-do-
	Annual Income	-do-
	Training	Scale developed for the study
	Social participation	Scale developed by Kamarudeen (1981)
	Extension participation	Scale developed by John (1991)
	Mass media contact	Scale developed by Jayalakshmi (1996)
	Credit Orientation	Scale developed for the study
	Attitude towards Self-employment	Scale developed by Jayalakshmi (2001)
	Decision making in family and community	Scale developed for the study
	Perception about self-help groups	Scale developed by Meera (2001)
	Self-esteem	Scale developed for the study
	Como politeness	Scale developed by Jayalakshmi (2001)
	Economic empowerment	Scale developed for the study
	Employment generation	
	Increase in income	Scaled developed by Jayalakshmi (2001) with slight modifications
	Economic motivation	Scale developed by Nanjaiyan
2.	Dependent Variables (Components of Empowerment)	
	Achievement Motivation	Scale developed by Singh (1970)

Contd....

1	2	3
	Risk taking Ability	Scale developed by Gangadharan (1993)
	Decision making ability	Scale developed by Ravichandran (1992)
	Management orientation	Scale developed by Samantha (1977)
	Initiativeness	Scale developed for the study
	Self-confidence	Scale developed by Nizamudeen (1996)
3.	Group Variables	
	Group interaction	Scale developed for the study
	Group motivation	-do-
	Need satisfaction	-do-
	Equity	-do-
	Group goal achievement	-do-
	Transparency	Scale developed by Sreedharan (1997)
	Interpersonal communication	Scale developed for the study
	Group leadership	-do-
	Interpersonal trust	-do-
	Team spirit	-do-
	Accountability	-do-

Based on the objectives, review of literature, discussion with experts and observations made by the researcher, a list of components of empowerment, group characteristics and personal, socio-psychological and economic variables were formed along with their operational definitions and the scores were assigned as follows.

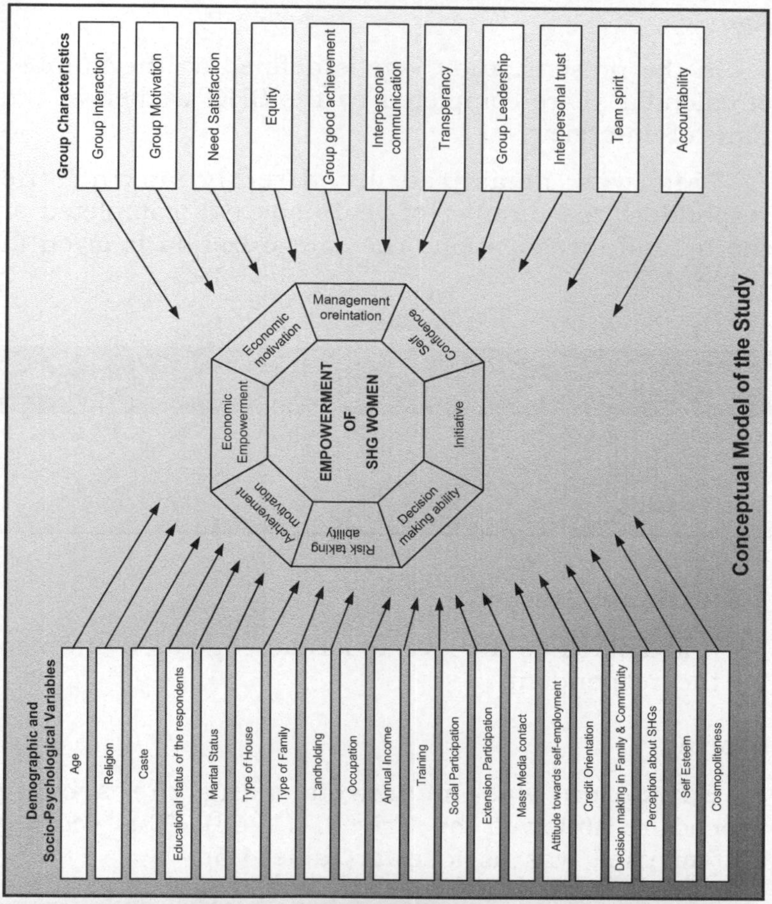

Conceptual Model of the Study

Response	Score
Most relevant	5
More relevant	4
Undecided	3
Less relevant	2
Least relevant	1

A. Socio-demographic and psychological variables

Age

In the present study, age is defined as the number of calendar years completed by the SHG women at the time of interview.

This was measured by directly asking the respondent the number of years she has completed at the time of investigation. The categorization is given in Table 4.5.

Table 4.5

Category	Age Group
Young	18 – 30
Middle	31 – 50
Old	Above 50

Educational Status

It is defined as the level of formal education attained by the respondent.

Scoring

Education was measured using the scoring procedure followed by Trivedi (1963). The scoring system used was as follows (Table 4.6).

Table 4.6

Category	Score
Illiterate	0
Can read only	1
Can read and write	2
Primary level	3
Middle level	4
High School	5
College and above	6

Educational Status of the Family

It is defined as the level of formal education attained by the members of the family.

The same procedure used by Trivedi (1963) was followed in this study for measuring the different levels of educational status of the family.

Occupation

Occupation is defined as the position of the family which acts as a source of income in which she spends major part of her time and attention.

Table 4.7

Category	Score
Self-employment	4
Farming	3
Labourers	2
Any others	1

Landholding

Landholding refers to the total land owned by the SHG women.

Scoring

This variable was measured by directly asking the respondents the total land possessed by them. The respondents were categorised in Table 4.8.

Table 4.8

Landholding	Score
5 – 10 cents	1
Above 10 – 15 cents	2
15 cents and above	3

Annual Income

Annual income is defined as the total earnings of the family for one year. This was obtained by adding the income earned by all adult members of the family and income from land for one year.

Scoring

The scoring procedure was as follows (Table 4.9).

Table 4.9

Category	Score
Rs. 10,000 – 25,000	1
Abvoe Rs. 25,000 – 35,000	2
Rs. 35,000 and above	3

Social Participation

Kamarudeen (1981) defined social participation as participation of individual in various formal social institutions either as a member or as an office bearer.

Scoring

Social participation was measured using the scale developed by Kamarudeen (1981). This scale was having two dimensions namely membership in organisations and participation in organisational activities. The scores were assigned in Table 4.10.

Table 4.10

Category	Score
No membership in any organisation	0
Membership in each organisation	1
Office bearer in each organisation	2

The scores obtained by a respondent on the above two dimensions were summed up across each item for all the organizations, which give the social participation score. The maximum possible score ranges from 0 to 20.

Training

It is operationally defined as the number of training in various production activities undergone by the respondent during the last three years.

Scoring

The scoring procedure rages from 0 to 3 (Table 4.11).

Table 4.11

Training Undergone	Score
No training	0
One training	1
Two training	2
Three or more trainings	3

Extension Participation

It was operationally defined as the extent of participation by a group member in various extension programmes/activities conducted in the area. Extension participation was measured using the procedure followed by John (1991). The participation of each respondent in extension programme whenever conducted during the previous year was used to arrive at extension participation score.

Table 4.12

Frequency	Score
Always attended	2
Sometimes attended	1
Never	0

Mass Media Contact

Mass media contact is operationally defined as the extent to which a rural women is exposed to different mass media communications such as radio, newspaper and television.

In the present study, Mass Media contact was measured using the scale adopted by Jayalakshmi (1996). The respondents were asked whether they have contact with the various mass media and the following score was adopted, for yes '1' and for no '0'

Attitude Towards Self-employment

Attitude towards self-employment is operationally defined as the degree of positive or negative feeling of rural women towards self-employment in the present study, attitude towards self employment was measured using the scale developed by Jayalakshmi (2001). The schedule consists of 10 statements. The responses were collected using a five point continuum. The scoring pattern of five, four, three, two and one were assigned respectively for positive statements and reversed for negative statements. Total score over all the ten statements was the respondent's score on attitude towards self-employment.

Perception about Self-help Groups

Refers to the recognition of the stimuli and the interpretation about Self-help groups by the respondents.

It was measured by applying the schedule developed by the researcher for the purpose. The schedule consists of six statements, out of which five were positive and one was negative, reflecting the respondents perception about self-help groups. The respondents were asked to give their responses in a five point continuum as 'Strongly agree', 'Agree', 'Undecided', 'Disagree' and

'Strongly disagree'. The scoring pattern of five, four, three, two and one were assigned respectively for positive statements and reversed for negative statements. Total score over all the six statements was the respondent's score on perception about self-help groups.

Credit Orientation

Credit orientation is operationally defined as the favourable and positive attitude of an individual SHG women towards obtaining credit from institutional sources for self-employment. The responses were collected using a five point continuum. The scoring procedure reversed for negative statements.

Cosmopoliteness

Cosmopoliteness is operationalized as the degree to which a rural women is oriented to her immediate outside social system. In this study the respondents were asked whether they have visited the neighbouring village/town. The responses were collected in a dichotomous pattern 'Yes' or 'No' to which score of 1 and 0 were assigned respectively to measure the frequency of visit the following scoring pattern was used. Most frequently '3', frequently '2', sometimes '1' and Never '0'. If the visit for personal purpose, a score of '2' and for entertainment a score of '1' was given. The individual scores were calculated by summing up the score.

Employment Generation

It refers to the extent to which the activities of self-help groups generated additional employment opportunities.

In this study, employment generation was measured by considering the number of man days of employment generated per year as members of SHGs. The scoring procedure developed by Jayalakshmi (2001) was used to measure with slight modification.

Table 4.13

Sl. No.	Employment generated in terms of No. of Mandays / year	Before joining SHGs	After joining SHGs	Score
1.	Up to 100 days			1
2.	100 – 200 days			2
3.	200 – 300 days			3
4.	Above 300 days			4

Increase in Income

Increase in income refers to the increase in family income as a result of being a member of self-help groups. The measurement of increase in income was done by asking the SHG members to state the increase in total income after joining in the self-help groups. The scoring procedure developed by Jayalakshmi (2001) was used to measure this variable, with modification.

Table 4.14

Sl. No.	Increase in Income in rupees per annum	Score
1.	Up to Rs. 500	1
2.	Rs. 500 – 1000	2
3.	Rs. 1000 – 2000	3
4.	Above 2000	4

Economic Motivation

It is operationally defined as an individuals orientation towards maximum economic gains. It was measured using a scale developed by Nanjaiyan (1985) with slight modifications. The scoring system is given in Table 4.15.

Table 4.15

Category	Score				
	SA	A	UN	DA	SDA
Positive Statement	5	4	3	2	1
Negative Statement	1	2	3	4	5

Components of Empowerment

A Likert type five-point scale was prepared and used to obtain the data on components of empowerment. This scale was developed by the researchers, and was translated into Telugu and Malayalam, the English version.

The scale consists of positive and negative statements. For each of the positive items on the scale are assigned a weightage ranging from five (Strongly agree) to one (Strongly disagree). Both three points and five-point scale were used to collect the information.

In case of negative items, the scoring scheme is reversed from one (Strongly agree) to five (Strongly disagree). The scoring key with the positive and negative items of the scale are given in Table 4.16.

Table 4.16: Scoring Scheme

Statements	Strongly Agree (SA)	Agree (A)	Undecided (U)	Disagree (D)	Strongly Disagree (SD)
Positive items	5	4	3	2	1
Negative items	1	2	3	4	5

The components of empowerment scores of a subject is the sum total of scores on the items on the scale a total score is obtained by summating the scores on individual items by the SHG women.

Achievement Motivation

It refers to the striving the respondents to do good work and attain a sense of accomplishment. Achievement motivation was measured using the scale developed by Singh (1970). The responses was collected on a five-point continuum.

Decision-making

In this study, decision-making pattern was referred as the nature of participation of self-help group members in making decisions. A SHG member may take independent decisions or consult her husband or family members or people other than family members to take decisions. The scale developed and adopted by Ravichandran (1992) was used in this study with suitable modifications.

Table 4.17

Type of decisions	Score
Joint decisions other then family members	1
Joint decisions with family members or husband	2
Independent decisions	3

Management Orientation

Management orientation refers to the degree to which a rural woman is oriented towards scientific management comprising of planning, production and marketing in their production unit.

Scoring

Management orientation was measured using the scale developed by Samantha (1977) with slight modification in the statements. The scale consists of 15 statements, five statements each for planning, production and marketing orientation. In each group positive and negative statements were mixed, the respondents were asked to state their agreement to each of the statements, and scores of 1 and 0 were assigned respectively considering whether statement is positive or negative.

Risk-taking Ability

It is defined as the degree to which a SHG women is oriented towards risk and uncertainty and have courage to face the problems in starting as income-generating activity. Risk taking ability was measured using the scale developed by Gangadharan (1993).

Scoring

The scale consists of six statements of which the fifth statement is negative. The responses were measured on a five-point continuum is given in Table 4.18.

Table 4.18

Response	Score
Strongly agree	5
Agree	4
Undecided	3
Disagree	2
Strongly disagree	1

Initiative

It is defined as the capacity of SHG women to come forward on her own to take up some activity. Initiative was measured using an arbitrary scale developed for the purpose. The scale consists of six statements. The respondents were asked to state their arrangement or disagreement to each of the statements and a score of

1 and 0 were assigned respectively for agreement and disagreement. In the case of negative statements the scoring pattern was reversed. Scores for each respondent was obtained by summation of the score of all six statements. The score ranges from 0 to 6.

Self-confidence

It refers to the extent of feeling of a SHG woman about her own powers, abilities and resourcefulness to perform any activity which she desires to undertake.

Scoring

This component was measured using the scale developed by Nizamudeen (1996). The scale consists of ten statements. The respondents were asked to state their agreement or disagreement to each of the statements and scores of 1 and 0 were assigned respectively considering whether the statement is positive or negative. The summation of the scores obtained by an individual indicate her level of self-confidence.

Based on the objectives of the study, review of literature, discussion with experts and after the pilot study, the following group characteristics like group interaction, group motivation, need satisfaction, equity, group goal achievement, interpersonal communication, transparency, group leadership, interpersonal trust, team spirit and accountability.

Table 4.19

Response	Score
Most relevant	5
More relevant	4
Undecided	3
Less relevant	2
Least relevant	1

The total scores obtained for each group characteristics were worked out. The variable having a relevancy score of 75 per cent and above were selected.

Group Characteristics Schedule

The schedule consists of information about the group. The group characteristics were measured using schedule developed by the researcher for the study. Some of the items were measured in three point continuum as 'always', 'sometimes' and 'never'. Positive scores carry of 'two', 'one' and zero. Negative statements carry scores of 'zero', 'one' and 'two', some of the items were measured using 5-point continuum.

Group characteristics were measured using schedule developed by the researcher for the study. The schedule of group interaction, group leadership need satisfaction, interdependence of members comprises of five statements each, and the schedule of transparency, accountability, team spirit and equity comprises of four statements each. Group leadership, transparency and accountability were measured in three point continuum as 'always', 'sometimes' and 'never'. Positive statements carry scores of 'two', 'one' and 'zero', and negative statements carry scores of 'zero', 'one' and 'two' respectively.

Group interaction, need satisfaction, team spirit, interpersonal of trust and equity were measured on a five point continuum ranging from 'strongly agree' to 'strongly disagree'. The scoring pattern ranged from 'fiver' to 'zero' for positive statements and 'zero' to 'five' for negative statements.

SCORING PROCEDURE

To find the group component score of each group (group characteristic values) the component score of each individual is calculated by dividing the obtained component score by maximum score possible for that group component, then multiplied by ten to get the group characteristic value. The group characteristic values of the group gives the group characteristic score.

Table 4.20: Maximum possible scores of SHGs on various dimensions regarding Socio-psychological status and components of empowerment of SHG members

Dimension	Number of Items	Scale Point	Score Range	
			Min	Max.
Social participation	2	3	0	3
Extension participation	5	3	0	5
Mass media contact	8	2	0	16
Decision making in family and community.	3	2	0	6
Credit orientation	4	5	1	5
Attitude towards self-employment	10	5	1	5
Perception about SHGs	6	5	1	5
Self-esteem	15	5	1	5
Cosmopoliteness	3	3	1	4
Employment Generation	5	5	0	5
Increase in Income	5	5	1	5
Economic Empowerment	5	3	1	5
Economic Motivation	5	5	1	5
Achievement Motivation	7	5	1	5
Management orientation	13	2	1	26
Decision-making ability	5	3	0	10
Risk-taking ability	6	5	1	5
Initiativeness	6	2	1	12
Self confidence	10	2	1	20

The responses from the SHG members regarding various dimensions has been classified into three levels, and the score in each dimension covered as listed in Table 4.20.

For each respondent the individual scores on each aspects have been summed in order to get a score for the dimensions under study.

Since the number of aspects in different dimensions is not the same, the score on each dimension has been categorized into three levels i.e., low, medium and high. Using the frequency distribution of the scores and the quartiles of the distribution, the classification has been made.

The impact of location Rural/Urban on each dimension and the levels (Low, medium, high) has been studied for the SHG groups in both the state. In each state the following null hypothesis is tested using chi-square test.

HO_1: The socio-economic and demographic status of the SHGs is independent of location.

HO_2 : The economic empowerment and the components of empowerment is independent of location.

HO_3: The group characteristics status is independent of location.

COLLECTION OF DATA

The data were collected by administering the schedule to the SHG women beneficiaries. The researcher established a good rapport with the respondents and explained the need of the study in which they have to respond to the items. The investigator collected the information from the illiterate respondents by conducting interviews with them. For the present study information from primary and secondary sources were selected. The information relating to number of women SHGs, number of groups and their involvement in income generating activities in the selected villages and mandals were collected from the records of Mandal office, DRDA office, municipal office etc.

STATISTICAL TECHNIQUES USED FOR THE STUDY

In view of the objectives cited the collected information was suitably inferred by calculating the following statistical constants. Besides simple methods of analysis like mean, percentages, standard deviation, other statistical tools like t-test, chi–square and ANOVA were also used. Paired 't'-test was used to test the significance between two averages of increase in income of respondents before and after joining in self-help groups. The next chapter deals with results and discussion.

CHAPTER 5

SOCIO-DEMOGRAPHIC AND PSYCHOLOGICAL CHARACTERISTICS OF THE RESPONDENTS

SECTION I

This chapter presents the findings of the research study. It has been divided into five sections. Section I deals with the findings of socio-demographic and psychological characteristics of SHG respondents. Section II is devoted to the findings of economic empowerment. Section III examines the components of empowerment. Section IV deals with the effect of age and education on socio-psychological variables and components of empowerment, Section V is devoted to the findings of the group variables.

For countless centuries women in India have been subordinated to men and socially oppressed. The various religious practices in India as well as the personal laws based on them, confined women to a status inferior to that of men. But Self-help groups are steadily bringing a silent revolution in the empowerment of women.

Self-help group are key elements for the empowerment of rural women which help them to improve their socio-demography conditions and possession of small credit assets. In the present study, the socio-demographic and psychological status scale of the following items describes the distribution of SHG members by age, religion, caste, educational status, marital status, type of house, type of family, family size, land holding etc., and also the level of participation of SHG members in various aspects like training, social participation, extension participation, mass media contacts, decision-making in family and community, attitude towards self-employment, Credit orientation, Perception about SHGs, Self-esteem, Cosmopoliteness for the 400 respondents who were selected from Madanapalle block in Chittoor district of Andhra Pradesh and Ottapalam block of Palakkad district, Kerala. The sample comprises of SHG women of DWCRA-SGSY, DWCUA-SJSRY groups from rural and urban areas.

Age

Age is one of the important variables in the understanding of an individuals location and status in the society. The sample constituted women of 18 years and above. The detail break up of the sample by age is given in Table 5.1 and Fig. 5.1.

Table 5.1: Percentage distribution of the respondents by Age

Age(in yrs)	Andhra SHGs		Kerala SHGs	
	Rural	Urban	Rural	Urban
18 - 30	33	39	14	23
31 - 50	67	59	71	63
Above 50	-	2	15	14
Total	100	100	100	100

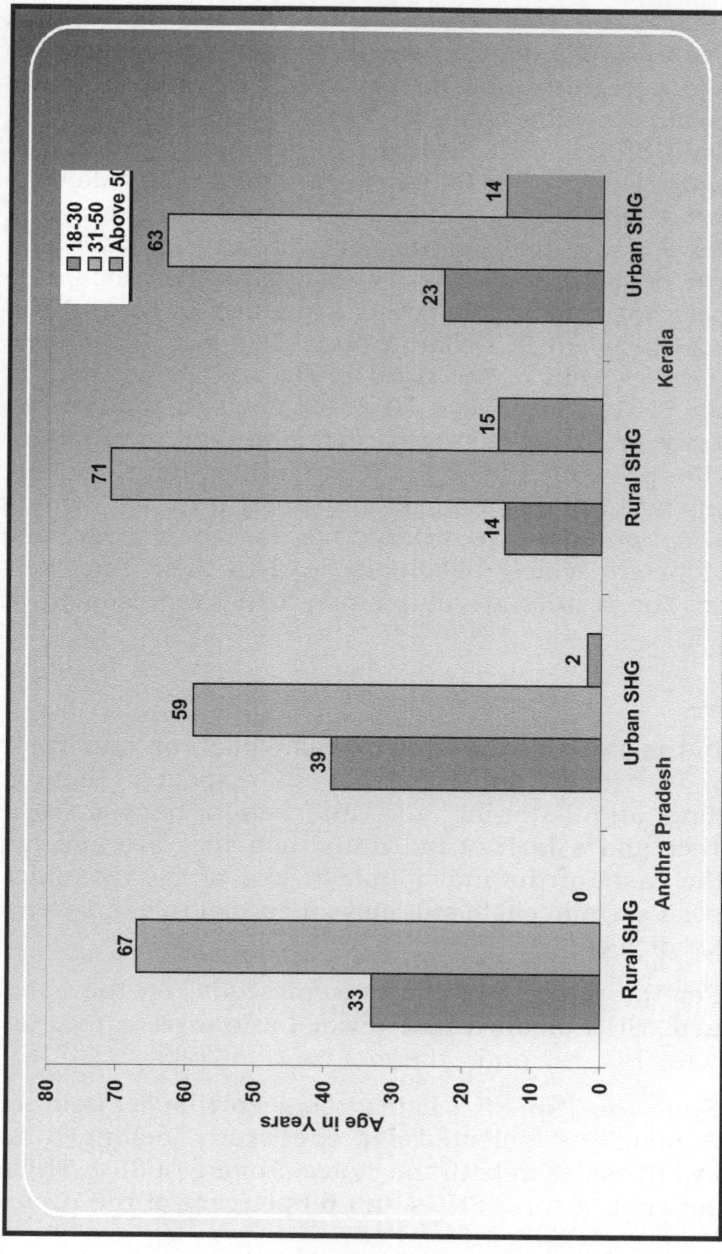

Fig.5.1: Percentage Distribution of the Respondents by Age

It may be seen from Table 5.1 that in Andhra Pradesh 67 per cent of the rural women belonged to middle age group and 33 per cent belonged to young age group, in urban area 59 per cent belonged to middle age and 39 per cent belonged to young age group and a negligible per cent, (2%) belonged to old age. Majority of the respondents in Kerala SHGs were in the age of 31-50 years, of that 71 per cent were in rural area and 63 per cent were in urban areas, while the remaining 14 per cent belonged to young age group in rural SHGs and 23 per cent in urban groups. It may also be seen that 15 per cent of the rural SHGs and 14 per cent of urban SHGs were above 50 years. In both the groups, majority of SHGs belonged to middle age group. Also in the present scenario of unemployment, people belonging to young and middle age group are coming forward prepared to take risks for their economic development which will finally lead to their empowerment. The results are diagrammatically represented in Fig. 5.1.

Caste

In the Indian social system, caste plays an important role. The individual behaviour in respect of eating, reading and listening and interaction between one another and a host of individual activities are affected by the caste of the individual. Inspite of the dynamics of social system, caste still plays a crucial role in several walks of life.

For the purpose of the present study, on the basis of caste, SHG members are divided into three categories viz, OC, BC, SC and others.

From the Table 5.2 it may be seen that majority of SHG members selected for the study belonged to backward castes in both the states. Among Andhra SHGs 79 per cent of rural SHGs and 63 per cent of the urban

SHGs were from backward castes while the remaining SHGs belonged to OC (6%) in rural and (27%) in urban groups where as 15 and 10 per cent belonged to SC category. In Kerala, 49 per cent of Rural SHGs and 64 per cent of urban SHGs belonged to backward castes followed by 35 per cent rural and 20 per cent from urban SHG groups belongs to scheduled caste. Consequently, the members profile indicates the same pattern of more number of members from backward castes followed by SCs and other castes.

Table 5.2: Percentage distribution of the respondents by Caste

Caste	Andhra SHGs		Kerala SHGs	
	Rural	Urban	Rural	Urban
OC	6	27	16	16
BC	79	63	49	64
SC / ST	15	10	35	20
Total	100	100	100	100

Religion

Like the caste, religion is also a powerful and influential force with a significant effect on the human behaviour. In India, majority of the people belongs to Hindu religion. The other religions includes Christians, Muslims, Sikhs and Buddhists. Hence, for the purpose of the study, the respondents were divided into three religious groups viz., Hindus, Muslims and Christians.

The data in Table 5.3 show the distribution of SHG women by their religion. It may be seen from the data in both the States of Andhra Pradesh and Kerala, majority of the respondents selected for the study were Hindus i.e., 94 per cent in rural and 78 per cent in urban Andhra Pradesh, and 93 per cent in rural and

91 per cent in urban Kerala. On the other hand 23 per cent from Andhra Pradesh and 15 per cent from Kerala was Muslims and only negligible percentage (5%) of SHGs members in Andhra Pradesh were Christians.

Table 5.3: Percentage distribution of respondents by Religion

Religion	Andhra SHGs		Kerala SHGs	
	Rural	Urban	Rural	Urban
Hindus	94	78	93	91
Muslims	1	22	7	8
Christians	5	-	-	1
Total	**100**	**100**	**100**	**100**

Educational Status

Education is the key which opens the door to life, develops humanity and promotes national development. Education can be an effective tool for women's empowerment. It enables rural women to acquire new knowledge and technology required for improving and developing their tasks in all fields.

In order to understand the role of education and participation in SHG, data pertaining to level of education of SHG members was collected and presented in Table 5.4.

The results indicate that in Andhra Pradesh 22 per cent of rural SHGs had high school education while three-fourths of the respondents had below high school education. In case of urban SHGs 55 per cent had high school education and remaining (45%) had less than high school education and on the whole a greater proportion (31%) of rural SHGs, and a small proportion of urban SHGs in Andhra Pradesh were illiterates. It is noticed that among Kerala SHGs 57 per cent of rural

SHGs and 42 per cent in urban SHGs had high school education. A very small per cent of (3%) rural and (2%) in urban SHGs were illiterates. Kerala is a State with total literacy and education up to primary level is free and compulsory, and females are given equal opportunity with that of males. Hence, the trend could be seen in the results. The results are depicted in Fig. 5.2.

Table 5.4: Percentage distribution of the respondents by Educational Status

Education	Andhra SHGs		Kerala SHGs	
	Rural	Urban	Rural	Urban
Illiterate	31	10	3	2
Read only	7	16	-	7
Read & Write	12	8	14	11
Primary school	28	11	26	38
High School & above	22	55	57	42
Total	100	100	100	100

Whereas in Andhra Pradesh SHGs the incidence of illiteracy was more, it may be recalled that out of 200 respondents, nearly 41 reported to be illiterate. It may also be observed that the participation in SHGs facilities access to literacy programmes that was in vogue in the district. Therefore, atleast one Functional literacy centre should be opened in each gram panchayat area with the objective of making all rural farm women functionally literate. The trend could be seen Fig. 5.2.

Marital Status

Marriage is considered to be a social obligation for women in Indian Society and the married are regarded with graceful status. Hence, the data pertaining to the

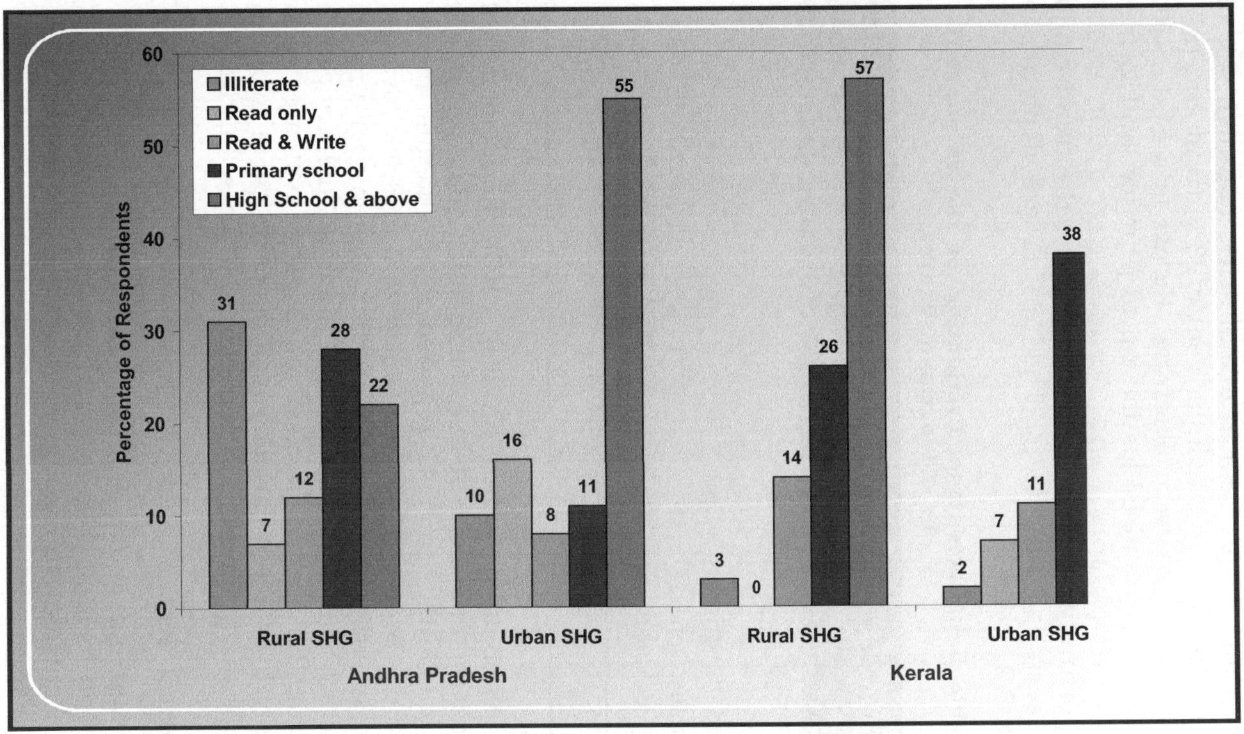

Fig.5.2: Percentage distribution of the respondents by Educational Status

marital status of the SHG women was also collected and presented in Table 5.5.

Table 5.5: Percentage distribution of respondents by Marital Status

Marital	Andhra SHGs		Kerala SHGs	
	Rural	Urban	Rural	Urban
Single/Unmarried	4	21	12	9
Married	93	74	76	76
Widowed	3	1	7	10
Divorce	-	4	5	5
Total	**100**	**100**	**100**	**100**

In Andhra SHGs, 93 per cent of Rural SHG members were married and among the married three per cent were widows, and a negligible per cent (4%) were unmarried. Among urban SHGs, 74 per cent were married, 21 per cent were unmarried, four of them were separated and only one member reported as widowed. In Kerala SHGs, 76 per cent of each of the urban and rural SHG women were married, while the remaining 12 rural and 9 were unmarried. Twelve rural and 15 urban respondents were neither separated nor widowed.

Type of House

Ownership of a house of any type gives a sense of security and belonging to the members. House is a source of self-esteem and dignity to the members. Ownership of a house promotes sanitation and healthy upbriging of children. The respondents were distributed by type of house they owned and was presented in Table 5.6.

The data show that a greater proportion of the respondents in both the States were living in tiled houses, while the remaining 21 per cent of rural SHG,

57 per cent of urban SHGs in A.P. 11 per cent rural and 38 per cent of urban SHGs in Kerala were living in pucca houses, where as a negligible per cent (5%) in Andhra Pradesh and 10 per cent in Kerala (both rural and urban together) linked in kachcha houses. In Kerala, Vambhay Valmiki Ambedkar Awas Yojana sanctioned house loans for Kudumbasree groups who were below poverty line, for the families who do not have houses and house-holds having only four cents of own land. In Andhra Pradesh, similar scheme was introduced by the Congress Government as 'Indira Grihanirmana Padhakamu' for those families of BPL groups.

Table 5.6: Percentage distribution of respondents by Type of House

Type of House	Andhra SHGs		Kerala SHGs	
	Rural	Urban	Rural	Urban
Pucca	21	57	11	38
Tiled	74	43	82	59
Kutcha	5	-	7	3
Total	100	100	100	100

Type of the Family

The type of family refers to the family being nuclear or joint or extended. The joint family system is a characteristic feature of the Indian Society, which is a very old institution of India. A joint family generally has an elderly male as the head of the family and other male and female members are subordinates to him. In other words, joint family is composed of two or more couples and their children including older persons related to them. The nuclear family is defined as the family consisting of husband, wife and unmarried children. The joint and extended family system is disintegrated due to increase in population and the spread of individualistic ideas in India.

SHG respondents selected for the study were divided according to their family type and three major family structures were observed in the study area i.e., Nuclear, joint and extended type. The results are depicted in Fig 5.3.

Table 5.7: Percentage distribution of the respondents by Type of Family

Type of Family	Andhra SHGs		Kerala SHGs	
	Rural	Urban	Rural	Urban
Pucca	21	57	11	38
Nuclear	64	70	80	83
Joint	28	24	18	13
Extended	8	6	2	4
Total	100	100	100	100

The data reveal that predominant number of respondents in both the states (64 rural and 70 per cent urban in Andhra Pradesh and 80 rural and 83 per cent urban SHGs in Kerala) were reported to be nuclear families and 28 and 24 per cent in Andhra Pradesh had joint families while a negligible per cent (8 and 6%) belonged to extended families. Among Kerala SHGs 18 and 13 per cent were from joint family system and 2 and 4 per cent were from extended families. It may be concluded that people are influenced by the individualistic ideas and opt for nuclear family system.

Family Size

Since the type of family provides only a social phenomena, an attempt has also been made to collect information on number of members in a given family of the respondents so that the influence of family size

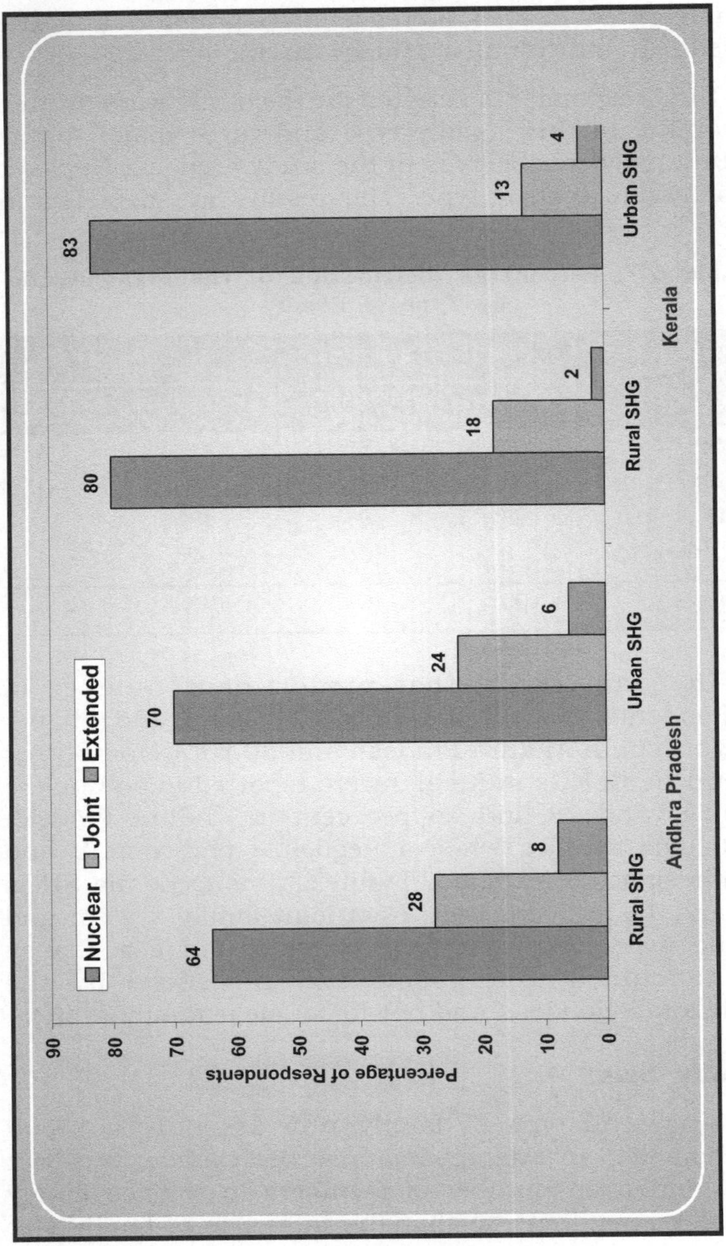

Fig.5.3: Percentage distribution of the respondents by Type of Family

on different aspects related to SHGs can be observed. The data was analysed in this regard and is presented in Table 5.8.

Table 5.8: Percentage distribution of respondents by Family Size

Family Size	Andhra SHGs		Kerala SHGs	
	Rural	Urban	Rural	Urban
Below 4	54	58	62	70
5 - 6	44	27	34	27
Above 6	2	15	4	3
Total	100	100	100	100

It may be seen that a higher percentage of the respondents in both the States had 1-4 members in their family. i.e., 54 and 58 per cent in Andhra Pradesh, 62 and 70 per cent among Kerala SHGs 47 and 27 per cent in Andhra Pradesh and 34 and 27 per cent in Kerala had 5-6 members in their households and a negligible 2 per cent and 15 per cent among urban SHGs in A.P. while in Kerala 4 and 3 per cent had above 6 members in their households. The results also indicate that majority of the respondents had less than 4 members in the family 34 and 27 per cent in Kerala, as the joint and extended family system was being eroded and nuclear family set up were on the increase.

Land-holding

Land adds to the economic and social status of the persons. The respondents were divided based on the land holdings and is presented in Table 5.9.

With regard to landholding, it is clear from Table 5.9 that majority of the respondents among Andhra Pradesh SHGs (93 & 67%) and 66 and 76 per cent of the Kerala SHG members were possessing land below five cents, and a negligible per cent (4 & 7%) in Andhra Pradesh and 11 per cent in Kerala had above 10 cents. The remaining 3 and 26 per cent of Andhra Pradesh SHGs and 34 and 13 per cent of Kerala SHGs, respondents were owning land between 5 to 10 cents.

Table 5.9: Percentage distribution of respondents by Land-holding

Land-holding	Andhra SHGs		Kerala SHGs	
	Rural	Urban	Rural	Urban
Below 5 cents	93	67	66	76
5-10 cents	3	26	34	13
Above 10 cents	4	7	-	11
Total	100	100	100	100

Occupational Status of Husbands

Occupation is regarded as an indicator of social status. The nature of occupation and the degree of participation in the respective occupations, however, decides the level of social status of an individual. Occupational status was divided into three categories viz., Agricultural labourers, non-agricultural labourers, business and others. Data on occupational status is presented in Table 5.10.

The major source of income of SHG households was from the nature of work of the male members i.e., husband, father or children undertaken in the family. The data in Table 5.10 show that among Andhra Pradesh SHGs, more than three-fourths of the respondent's spouses were non-agricultural labourers like coolies, masons and labourers in construction work. More than half of the respondent's spouses (18 & 46%) were engaged in business, specifically in weaving and handlooms. The remaining 29 per cent of the rural

SHG spouses and 12 per cent urban SHGs were engaged in farming and agricultural activities. In kerala, among rural SHGs 42% of rural SHG spouses were engaged in agricultural operations followed by 38 per cent in non-agricultural activities and 20 per cent in business and other activities. Among urban SHGs 38% were agricultural labourers followed by 24 per cent in business and the remaining 49 per cent in non-agricultural labourers.

Table 5.10: Percentage distribution of respondents by Occupational Status of the husbands

Occupational Status of husband/others	Andhra SHGs		Kerala SHGs	
	Rural	Urban	Rural	Urban
Farming/ Agricultural labourers	29	12	42	38
Non-Agricultural labourer (coolie, masson, etc.)	53	34	38	49
Business & Others	18	46	20	24
Total	**100**	**100**	**100**	**100**

Annual Income

The financial status of the family plays an important role to play in terms of participation of self-help groups, and as such an attempt has been made to collect the information on yearly income status of the respondents selected for the study and is presented in Table 5.11.

It was found that slightly more than three-fourths of the Andhra Pradesh respondents were having an income between Rs.10,000 to 25,000 per annum, followed by 32 members whose income was between Rs.25,000-35,000 and only seven respondent's income was above Rs.35,000 per annum. In Kerala, of the total rural SHG members 70 per cent had a family income of Rs.10,000-25,000 per annum followed by 26 per cent whose income ranges from Rs.25,000 to Rs.35,000 and only 4 per cent of the respondent's income was above Rs.35,000. Among urban SHGs 78 per cent of the SHG members income ranged between Rs.25,000-35000, 10 per cent of the SHG members income was above Rs.35,000.

Table 5.11: Percentage distribution of respondents by Annual Income

Annual Income (in Rs.)	Andhra SHGs		Kerala SHGs	
	Rural	Urban	Rural	Urban
10,000 - 25,000	81	80	70	78
25,000 - 35,000	12	20	26	12
Above 35,000	7	-	4	10
Total	100	100	100	100

It may be recalled that members having income below Rs.18,000 are often considered as people living under BPL, category and also people having the income up to Rs.24,000 (per annum) were also considered as poor. Keeping this in view, it may be concluded that majority of the respondents both in Andhra Pradesh and Kerala belonged to very poor and poor households. Thus, SHGs like DWCRA/SGSY has been successful attracting the attention of poor and very poor households in the study area.

Training

It refers as the number of trainings in various production activities undergone by the SHG beneficiaries during the last three years. Emphasis is laid on training programme of functionaries under the

DWCRA. Rural development institutes at the central level like NIRD, at the State level APARD and at the district T.T.D.C provides training facilities for the SHGs respondents.

Table 5.12: Percentage distribution of respondents by number of training programmes attended

Training	Andhra SHGs		Kerala SHGs	
	Rural	Urban	Rural	Urban
One Training	54	20	45	30
Two Training	20	40	30	10
Three or more	26	40	25	60
Total	100	100	100	100

The distribution pattern of the SHG members based on their training revealed that in the case of Andhra Pradesh SHGs, nearly 54 per cent of rural SHGs attended one training and 20 per cent attended two trainings, 26 per cent attended more than three trainings programmes. In the urban SHGs, 40 per cent had attended two training and other 40 per cent attended more than three training programmes. Among Kerala SHGs, 45 per cent of rural SHGs attended one training, 30 per cent attended two trainings and 25 per cent participated in more than three training programmes. In the urban groups 60 per cent attended more than three trainings, 30 attended only one training programme and 10 per cent attended two training programmes.

Social Participation

Social participation is defined as the extent of participation in various formal social institutions either as a member or as an office bearer.

Table 5.13: Percentage distribution of the respondents by Social participation level

Social Participation	Andhra SHGs		Kerala SHGs	
	Rural	Urban	Rural	Urban
Member of one organization	99	100	91	96
Member of more than one organization	1	-	9	4
Total	100	100	100	100

With regard to social participation, it was found that 99 per cent of the rural SHG respondents among Andhra Pradesh were members of only one organization i.e., women SHG. Similarly cent per cent of the urban SHGs were members of one organization only. In Kerala, 91 per cent of Rural SHG members and 96 per cent of urban SHGs were members of one organization only. Against this nine per cent of rural SHGs and 4 per cent of urban SHGs were members of more than one organization like mahila mandals, farmer's associations.

Extension Participation

Extension participation was operationally defined as the extent of participation by SHG members in various extension programme/activities conducted in the area during the previous year. The participation of each respondent in extension programme whenever conducted during the previous year was used to arrive at extension participation score. The results were depicted in Fig 5.4.

It may be seen that the level of extension participation of rural and urban SHGs of Andhra and of Kerala SHGs was low.

Table 5.14: Percentage distribution of respondents by Extension Participation

Extension Participation	Andhra SHGs		χ^2	Kerala SHGs		χ^2
	Rural	Urban		Rural	Urban	
Low	91	46		74	49	
Medium	-	-	46.92*	-	-	13.198*
High	9	54		26	51	
Total	**100**	**100**		**100**	**100**	

* Significant at 0.05% level.

John (1991) found that mere membership in groups itself had enhanced the extension participation of the members and that extension participation had positive and significant influence on adoption of pepper cultivation practices.

Mass Media Contact

Mass media contact is operationally defined as the extent to which a rural women is exposed to different mass media communications such as Radio, newspaper and Television.

Table 5.15: Percentage distribution of respondents by mass media contact

Mass Media contract	Andhra SHGs		χ^2	Kerala SHGs		χ^2
	Rural	Urban		Rural	Urban	
Low	73	38	24.08*	45	31	4.16*
Medium	-	-		-	-	
High	37	62		55	69	
Total	**100**	**100**		**100**	**100**	

* Significant at 0.05% level.

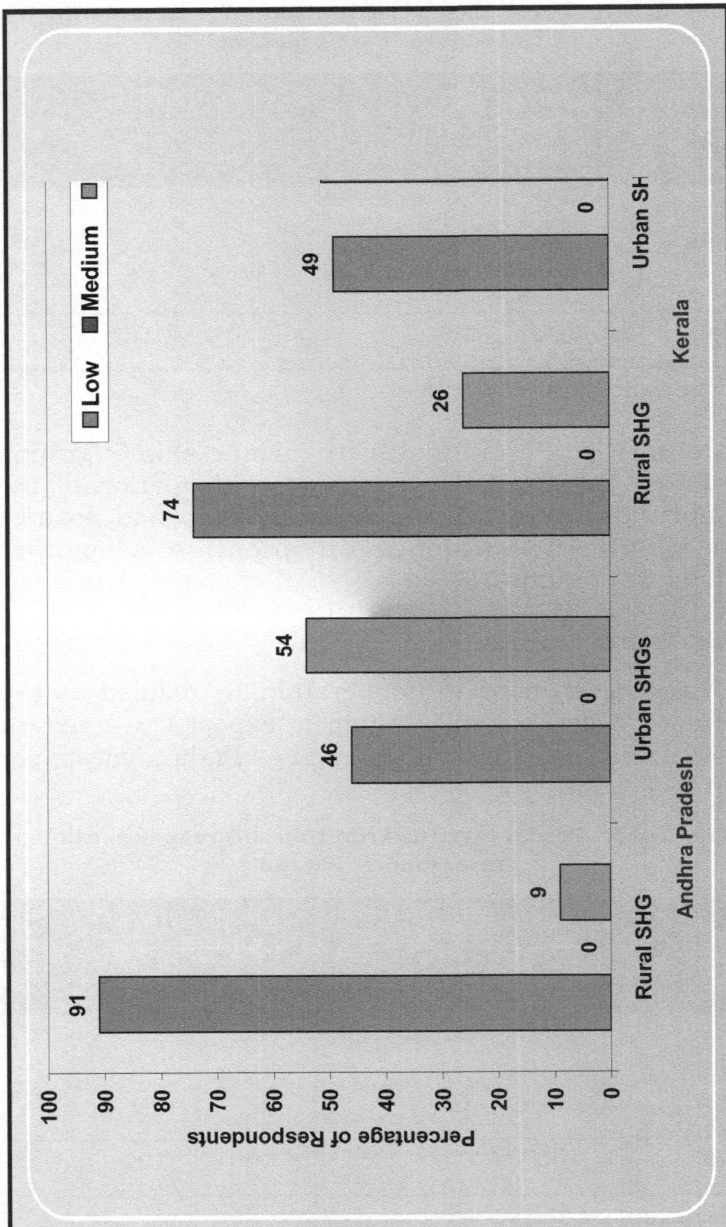

Fig.5.4: Percentage distribution of the respondents by extension participation

It could be seen from Table 5.15 that among Andhra SHGs 73 per cent of the rural SHGs have low mass media contact and more than one-fourth of the respondents 37 per cent had high mass media contact. In the case of Kerala SHGs, nearly half of rural SHGs (45%) had low mass media contact. There is much difference between rural and urban SHGs of Andhra Pradesh when compared with Kerala. Because of the high literacy rate in Kerala most of the households subscribed for atleast one news paper and every family possess radio or television and naturally their mass media contact will be high. The findings of the study is in line with that of Meera (2001).

Credit Orientation

Credit orientation is operationally defined as the favourable and positive attitude of an individual rural women towards obtaining credit from institutional sources for self-employment.

Table 5.16: Percentage distribution of respondents by credit orientation

Dimension	Andhra SHGs		χ^2	Kerala SHGs		χ^2
	Rural	Urban		Rural	Urban	
Low	41	34		17	15	
Medium	41	48	1.204@	46	47	1.149@
High	18	18		37	38	
Total	**100**	**100**		**100**	**100**	

@ Not significant.

The distribution pattern of the respondents based on their credit orientation revealed that in case of Andhra Self-help groups and Kerala self-help groups, there is no significant differences with regard to credit orientation. In case of Andhra Self-help groups, nearly

75 per cent of (both rural and urban SHGs) respondents had low credit orientation. Since credit orientation is an important precursor, all the groups have a fairly good representation.

Attitude towards Self-employment

Attitude towards self-employment is operationally defined as the degree of positive or negative feeling of rural women towards self-employment.

Table 5.17: Percentage distribution of respondents by attitude towards self employment

Attitude toward self-employment	Andhra SHGs		χ^2	Kerala SHGs		χ^2
	Rural	Urban		Rural	Urban	
Low	77	40		-	2	
Medium	23	60	28.195*	42	48	2.993@
High	-	-		58	50	
Total	**100**	**100**		**100**	**100**	

* Significant at 0.05% level; @ Not Significant.

A critical review of the data shows that among Andhra SHGs, majority of the rural SHGs got low scores with regard to attitude toward self-employment. In the case of Kerala SHGs no significant difference was found between urban and rural SHGs, with regard to attitude towards self-employment.

More than half of the respondents had high scores. In this present context of extreme unemployment, the only alternative for income generation is to take-up self-employment where initial investment is less and can be taken up with the available resources. The findings of the study are in line with that of Jayalakshmi (1996).

Decision-making in family and community

The respondents were distributed by decision making in family and community activities.

Table 5.18: Percentage distribution of respondents by decision making in family and community

Decision making in family and community	Andhra SHGs		χ^2	Kerala SHGs		χ^2
	Rural	Urban		Rural	Urban	
Low	42	34		32	38	
Medium	40	14	29.87*	38	31	1.241@
High	18	52		30	31	
Total	**100**	**100**		**100**	**100**	

* Significant at 0.05% level; @ Not Significant.

The data indicate that in case of decision making in family and community among Andhra rural SHGs, 42 per cent had low level of decision making in family and community followed by 40 per cent with medium level of decision-making and 18 per cent with high level of decision-making in family and community. Where as among urban SHGs, 52 per cent had high decision making in family and community and 34 per cent had low and 14 per cent had medium level of decision making capacity. There is no significant difference between Kerala rural and urban groups. Nearly three-fourths of the SHG members of Andhra Pradesh and 70 per cent SHGs of Kerala had low decision making in family and community. This may be due to the reason that the members of group might be far away from the sources of information along with their chances in meeting and contacting others. The trend is depicted in Fig. 5.5.

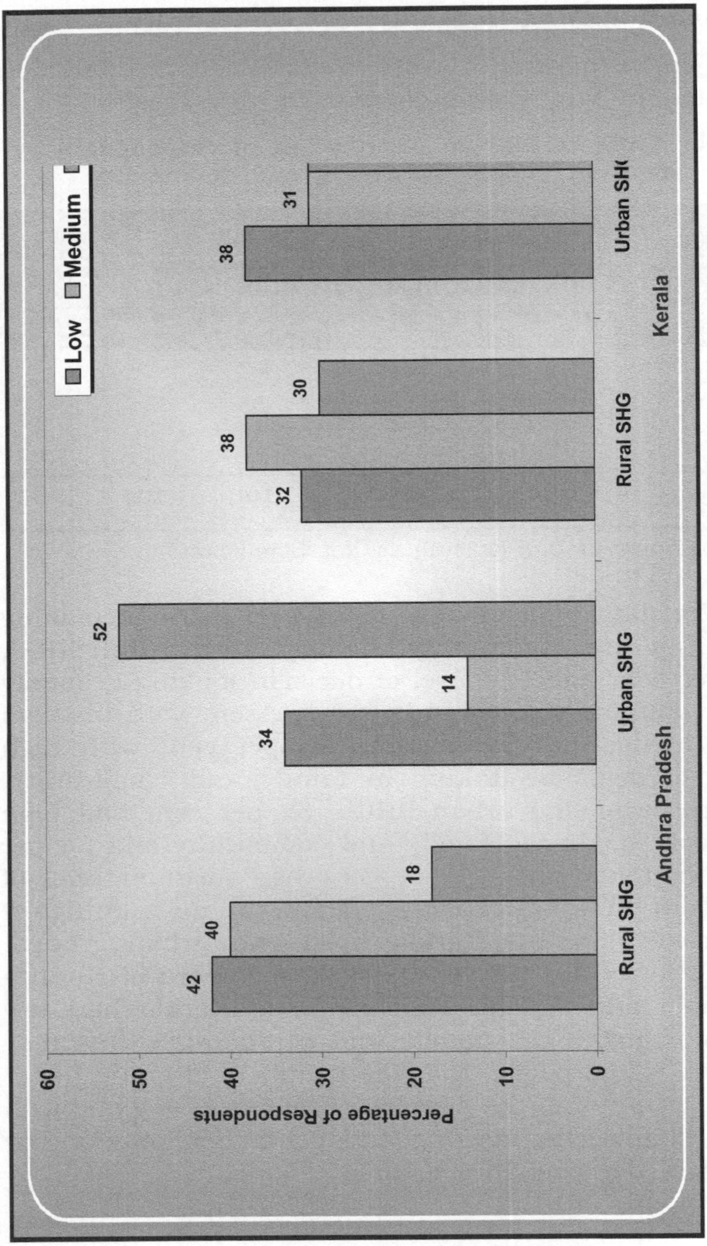

Fig.5.5: Percentage distribution of of the respondents by Decision making family and community

Perception about Self-help Groups

Perception is a process of becoming aware of objects or events by means of sensory operations.

Table 5.19: Percentage distribution of respondents by perception about self-help groups

Perception about self-help groups	Andhra SHGs		χ^2	Kerala SHGs		χ^2
	Rural	Urban		Rural	Urban	
Low	94	95		38	54	
Medium	-	-	0.96@	-	-	5.163@
High	6	5		62	56	
Total	**100**	**100**		**100**	**100**	

@ Not Significant.

Perusal of Table 5.19 reveals that majority of the Andhra Pradesh SHGs (94 & 95%) were in the low category and only a negligible per cent belonged to high perception score. As these rural women in Andhra Pradesh did not involve in any self-employment training programmes and hence had very low perception about self-help groups. They lack interest in attending training programmes. But in case of Kerala, more than half of the respondents (62 & 56%) had high scores. High perception about one's group, energises the group members to push the group to better stability. But the difference between the two groups is not significant. Table 18 presents the comparative view of the perception levels of the SHGs beneficiaries of both Andhra Pradesh and Kerala.

Self-esteem

Self-esteem was measured using a standardized instrument used by Seema (1997) with minor modification. The inventory was constructed making use of Self-reporting method.

Table 5.20: Percentage distribution of respondents by self-esteem

Self-esteem	Andhra SHGs		χ^2	Kerala SHGs		χ^2
	Rural	Urban		Rural	Urban	
Low	72	22		1	6	
Medium	23	73	58.46*	39	52	8.605@
High	1	5		60	42	
Total	**100**	**100**		**100**	**100**	

* Significant at 0.05% level; @ Not Significant.

A glance through Table 5.20 reveals that there is significant difference between Andhra Pradesh rural SHGs and Andhra urban SHGs with regard to Self-esteem score (72 & 22%). Most of the rural SHGs had low scores in Andhra Pradesh when compared with urban SHGs and 73 per cent of urban SHGs got medium scores, while only neglible per cent had high scores (1 and 5%). In Kerala SHGs, significant difference was not found between rural and urban SHGs. Majority of the respondents (60%) in rural SHGs got High scores as 42% in urban SHGs. A negligible per cent (1 and 6%) had low scores.

Cosmospoliteness

Cosmopoliteness is operationally defined as the degree to which a rural women is oriented to her immediate outside social system.

It is evident from the Table 5.21 that nearly half of the respondents of Andhra Pradesh SHGs got low scores with regard to cosmopoliteness and the remaining half of the respondents (48 & 50%) had high scores. Whereas among Kerala SHGs, more than half of the respondents i.e., 68 and 70 per cent had low scores and 32 per cent of rural SHGs and 30 per cent of urban SHGs got high scores. Cosmopoliteness refers to the tendency of the SHG members to be in contact with outside village on the belief that all the needs of an individual cannot be met within his own village.

Table 5.21: Percentage distribution of respondents by cosmopoliteness

Cosmopoliteness	Andhra SHGs		χ^2	Kerala SHGs		χ^2
	Rural	Urban		Rural	Urban	
Low	52	49		68	70	
Medium	-	-	0.125@	-	-	0.094@
High	48	50		32	30	
Total	**100**	**100**		**100**	**100**	

@ Not Significant.

Hence, the hypothesis that 'there is no significant difference in the socio-demographic and psychological characteristics of SHG women beneficiaries in Andhra Pradesh and Kerala', is rejected.

SUM UP

Majority (67% and 59%) of the rural and urban SHG respondents of Andhra Pradesh, 71 per cent and 63 per cent of rural and urban SHG respondents of Kerala were in the age group of 31-50 years. Majority (94% and 78%) of the SHG respondents in Andhra Pradesh, (93% and 91%) and of Kerala were Hindus. A high proportion (79% and 63%) of the SHG respondents in Andhra Pradesh and nearly half of the (49% and 64%) SHG respondents in Kerala belonged to backward castes.

Majority (79% and 45%) of the rural and urban SHG respondents in Andhra Pradesh had education below high school level. In case of Kerala, a comparatively small proportion (43% and 58%) had below high school education. About one-third in Andhra Pradesh (31%) of rural SHGs and 10 per cent of urban SHGs were illiterates. Kerala SHG respondents were better educated as compared to Andhra Pradesh SHG respondents.

Majority of the respondents (93% and 73%) of Andhra Pradesh SHGs (76%) of Kerala SHGs were married. A great proportion (74% and 43%) of Andhra Pradesh SHGs were living in tiled houses and among Kerala SHGs 82 per cent and 59 per cent were living in tiled houses.

A large proportion (64% and 70%) of Andhra Pradesh SHGs belonged to nuclear family system as more than three fourths (80% and 83%) of Kerala SHGs. Majority of (54% & 58%) of the respondents in Andhra Pradesh had below 4 members in their family and more than half (62% and 70%) of the respondents in Kerala had less than 4 members in the family.

A higher percentage (93% and 67%) of respondents in Andhra Pradesh and (66% and 76%) Kerala SHGs were possessing land below 5 cents. Majority (53% and 34%) of the respondent's spouses in Andhra Pradesh were non-agricultural labourers and in Kerala 38% and 49% were non-agricultural labourers. More than three-fourths (81% and 80%) of Andhra SHGs and (70% & 78%) Kerala SHGs had a family income of Rs.10,000-25,000 per annum.

More than one fourth (26% and 40%) of Andhra SHGs attended three or more training programmes and 25% and 60% of Kerala SHGs attended three or more training programmes. Majority (99%) of the Andhra SHGs (91 and 96%) of Kerala SHGs were members of one organization. A higher percentage (91% and 41%) had low level of extension participation among Andhra SHGs and among the Kerala SHGs, 74% and 59% had low level of extension participation. With regard to mass media contact, 73% and 38% of Andhra SHGs and 45 and 31% of Kerala SHGs had low level of mass media contact. Majority (41 and 48%) of Andhra and (46% each) Kerala SHGs had medium scores for credit orientation. A higher percentage of Andhra SHGs (77 and 40%) got low scores with regard to attitude towards self-employment and more than half (58 and 50%) of Kerala SHGs had positive attitude towards self-employment.

Nearly three-fourths (74%) of the Andhra Pradesh SHGs and 70 per cent of Kerala SHGs had low decision making in family and community. Majority (94 and 95%) of the Andhra Pradesh SHGs had low perception score while more than half (62 and 56%) of the respondents got high scores with regard to perception about self-help groups. A greater percentage (72 and 22%) of Andhra SHGs got low scores and among Kerala SHGs more than half (60%) of rural SHGs and 42% of urban SHGs in Kerala had high mean scores for self-esteem. With regard to cosmopoliteness nearly half of the respondents (52% and 49%) in Andhra Pradesh got low scores and among Kerala SHGs more than half of the respondents (68% and 70%) got low scores.

SECTION II

ECONOMIC EMPOWERMENT OF SELF-HELP GROUPS

> "When tiny, tiny things start happening a million times, it becomes a large thing. It lays down the foundation of a strong economic base. With women participating in building this economic base, it becomes the foundation for better social and economic future".
>
> - *Srinivas .H*

Economic empowerment and progress in any country could be achieved only if poor people could be organized into groups for assertion of various services related to their progress. This can be achieved through mobilization of thrift, easy credit, upgradation of services and improved income generation opportunities essential for emancipation of women. Credit needs of the rural women are fulfilled through providing economic assistance to them through Self-help groups. SHGs are an effective economic approach for ensuring access of credit to the poor and vulnerable sections of the society. Self-help groups is a form of association of like minded people who are coming together for economic activities.

The status of women is intimately connected with their economic position which in turn depends on opportunities for women in participating in economic activities. Women's ability to save and access to credit would give them an economic role not only within the household, but may be outside as well. Investment in economic activities of women would improve employment opportunities for women and their participation in decision making process with regard to raising and distribution of resources – income investment and expenditure. The basic objective of DWCRA-SHG is to promote income generating skills and activities among poor women in rural areas thereby improving their social and economic status. Promoting thrift and savings has been accepted as a key entry point activity to organize the women's groups and undertake economic activities.

Self-Help Groups and Economic Empowerment

The initial efforts of SHGs was to empower women economically. Economic empowerment means financial self reliance inside and outside the household. Economic empowerment is a key and may lead to all kind of development. Economic empowerment means not only creation of wealth, but also creation of peoples capacity to create wealth and this resides in their health, education, knowledge and skills. The succeeding chapter deals with the economic empowerment of SHG women in the States of Andhra Pradesh and Kerala.

Table 5.22: Percentage distribution of SHG respondents by economic empowerment

Economic Empowerment	Andhra SHGs		Kerala SHGs	
	Rural	Urban	Rural	Urban
Increase in women earning capacity	100	100	100	100
Improved financial status	100	100	100	100

Cent percent of the women respondents were of the view that SHGs had helped them in increasing their earnings and income levels. Only negligible per cent among rural and urban SHGs in Andhra Pradesh opined that they don't have financial support at house hold. Majority of the respondents in Kerala SHGs stated that SHGs helped to increase their financial status.

Table 5.23: Percentage distribution of SHG respondents by financial self-reliance

Level	Andhra SHGs		χ^2	Kerala SHGs		χ^2
	Rural	Urban		Rural	Urban	
Low	45	44	0.20@	36	42	0.757@
High	44	55		64	56	

@ Not Significant.

With regard to financial Self reliance, there is no significant difference between Andhra Pradesh and Kerala Self-help groups. It was noticed from both the groups, that nearly half of the respondents agreed that financial decisions were taken by their husbands, while the remaining reported that decisions were taken by both husband and wives (64 and 56). Women's participation in economic decision was a vital means by which their economic dependency and social inequality could be overcome.

Table 5.24: Percentage distribution of respondents by improved family living conditions after joining the SHG

Family living conditions	Andhra SHGs		Kerala SHGs	
	Rural	Urban	Rural	Urban
Improved	100	100	100	100
Not improved	-	-	-	-

A perusal of Table 9.24 reveals that all of the women respondents, were of the view that their family living conditions have improved after joining the SHGs. Majority of the respondents were utilizing the additional income for better food, consumption for the family and to educate their children. Only a small per cent of respondents were spending their additional income to purchase assets and perform marriage/functions.

Savings

Self-help groups through savings has been adopted as a mass movement by the rural women, a path chosen by them, to shape the future destiny. The World Bank Micro Credit Summit held in Washington (2001-02) has agreed that women's Self-help is one of the most important schemes to tackle socio-economic poverty.

According to an World Bank estimate, out of 10 million in the world who are carrying on thrift activity, two million were in Andhra Pradesh itself. There are about 4.75 lakhs SHGs working in the state with the main objective of improving the economic status of rural women and their children. The District Rural Development Agency (DRDA) in most of the districts are actively involved in transforming SHGs into savings and credit groups to generate self-employment opportunities.

Table 5.25: Financial assistance provided for promotion of savings and credit groups in Andhra Pradesh

Total assistance provided to savings & credit groups in Andhra Pradesh	Amount in Rs.
Total number of self-help groups	4.75 lakhs
Total advances to women groups	880 crores
Savings mobilized through SHGs	1600 crores
Total corpus funds released	640 crores
Total Number of women groups benefited	2.10 lakhs
Total Number of women benefited	26.5 lakhs

Source: Ministry of Rural development and Panchayat Raj, Government of A.P 2002.

One of the key objectives of DWCRA-SHG is to promote thrift among the members. Saving by each member is introduced as an entry point in the formation of groups. Apart from meeting, the immediate consumption needs, the Savings of the members is expected to become the seed money for investment to economic activities at a later stage. Therefore, regularity of savings as well as the amount saved is important for the group dynamics. Besides the utilization of the savings i.e., the number of times the amount is revolved, the rate of interest, the purpose for which the borrowed funds are utilized and the repayment assume importance in the context of successful group functioning.

Table 5.26: Percentage distribution of respondents by monthly savings

Family living conditions	Andhra SHGs		Kerala SHGs	
	Rural	Urban	Rural	Urban
Below 50	-	-	-	-
50 – 75	100	80	100	100
75 - 100		20	-	-
Total	100	100	100	100

Source: Collected from passbooks of SHG members 2003.

It can be observed from Table 5.26 that majority of the SHG members have their monthly savings of Rs. 50-75. In Andhra Pradesh, 20 urban SHGs members had a monthly savings of Rs. 75-100. At the initial stage they used to save the amount of Rs.50 per month, but after discussing with the leaders, the group decided to increase their monthly savings as Rs. 50-75 per month. All the SHG members in both the states agreed that the most striking advantage of the SHGs was the savings which help them to meet emergencies and acted as informal bank at their door step.

The economic activities under taken by the SHG members in the States of Andhra Pradesh and Kerala fall under following categories. In order to maintain uniformity, all the members drawn for the study were from among those SHGs which were atleast three years old, and effective by functioning. The sample selected for the study had various income generating activities and also members in self-employment groups.

Table 5.27: Economic Activities (Micro-enterprise) under taken by SHG respondents in Andhra Pradesh and Kerala

Location	Name of SHG	Type of Income generating activity	Source of loan
Andhra Pradesh			
Rural	DWCRA	Petty Shops, individual self-employment	Thrift/Bank
Urban	DWCUA – SJSRY	Handloom Units (2)	Thrift/Bank
		Handicrafts (1)	Thrift/Bank
		Soft toys (1)	Thrift/Bank
		Embroidery (1)	Thrift/Bank
Kerala			
Rural	DWCRA-SGSY	Dairy (2)	Govt/Thrift
		Tailoring & Redymade (1)	Thrift/Bank
		Palm leaf plate making (1)	Thrift/Bank
		Idol making (1)	Thrift/Bank
Urban	DWCUA	Vanitha Canteen (1)	Thrift/Bank
		Computer Unit (1)	Govt/Thrift
		Cleaning & Sanitation units (2)	Govt/Thrift

The initial investment for certain economic activities is much higher than the revolving fund amount given to the individual members. Since bank loan is also advanced to the members they are able to make some investment through the amount of revolving fund and many respondents were of the opinion that even if the assistance was less than actual requirement, it had improved their credit worthiness and consequently helped them in raising supplementary resources. The additional income generated would ultimately depend on the economic activity undertaken. The additional income generated would improve the access of the women to better nutrition, health care, general living conditions etc.

Employment Generation

The increase in income is a result of the changes in the occupational shift and employment of SHG members. A significant proportion of the respondents who were formerly housewives and employed marginally in household economic activities have taken up full time economic activities which yield additional employment and income. An examination of data in Table 5.28 reveals that there is significant occupational mobility in respect of the respondents, as a result of being a self-help group member of DWCRA, SGSY, SJSRY etc.

Employment Generation

The aggregate benefit of employment generation due to self-help Groups, in both the states irrespective of location (rural/urban) is shown in the Table 5.28.

The data in Table 5.28 reveal that majority of SHG beneficiaries in both the states of Andhra Pradesh and Kerala had an increase in employment generation after joining in Self-help groups. Majority of the (62%) respondents of Andhra Pradesh had less than 100 days of employment per annum, 17 per cent had 101-200 days of employment in a year, and 21 per cent had above 200 days per annum (Fig. 5.6). Among Kerala SHGs. 36 per cent had an employment of less than 100 days followed by 35 per cent between 101-200 days per annum and 29 per cent above 200 days. After joining in self help groups, both Andhra SHGs and Kerala SHGs had increased their additional employment for more than 200 days per annum.

Table 5.28: Percentage distribution of respondents by employment generation (Number of days per annum)

Employment Generation	Andhra SHGs			Kerala SHGs		
No. of days per annum	0-100	101-200	201-300	0-100	101-200	201-300
Before joining in SHGs	123(62)	34(17)	43(21)	72(36)	71(35)	57(29)
After joining in SHGs	28(14)	15(7)	157(79)	21(10)	15(8)	164(82)

Figures in parentheses are the percentages.

From the Table 5.28, it is also clear that members who were employed for less than 100 days in a year had moved to higher employment groups after joining DWCRA – SHG activities. DWCRA, SGSY and SJSRY had contributed to the employment of SHG members for more than 200 days. The additional employment generated by SHGs appears to be responsible for the additional income generated. The results are depicted in Fig.5.6.

Increase in Income

In India, annual income of the family has been considered as the sole parameter to detect poverty. But this opaque indicator is just one among the numerous causes for the curse called poverty. The income

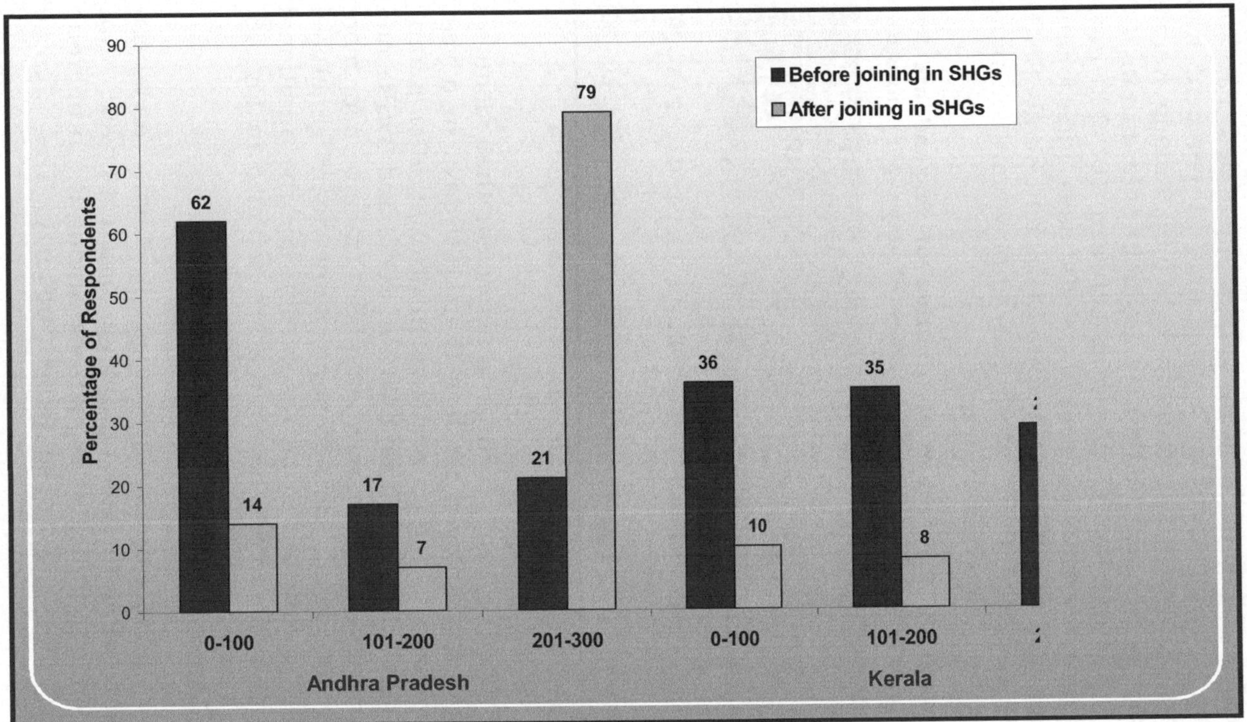

Fig. 5.6: Percentage distribution of the respondent by Employment Generation

columns of ration cards invariably tell wrong stories. More over income based surveys to identify poverty give the bureaucracy ample room for favouritism and corruption.

Poverty detection – 'The nine-factor risk index' of Kudumbashree SHGs: Kutcha house, No access to safe-drinking water, No access to sanitary latrine, illiterate adult in the family, Family having not more than one earning member, Family getting barely two meals a day or less, Presence of children below 5 years in the family, Alcoholic or drug addict in the family, Scheduled caste or tribe in the family.

Families that emit red signals to at least four out of the above nine risk factors will come under the category of "high risk poor families". Even the chosen risk factors have been envisaged as flexible one's as the situation prevailing in different regions of the state differ.

Increase in Income – Andhra Pradesh SHGs

Earning money give an economic independence to a women to do purchase or to spend money according to her own interest, requirements of children and their family. Further, it supplements the income and improves the standard of living.

From Table 5.29 it can be seen that there is no significant difference in the level of income after joining self-help groups among rural SHG members of DWCRA groups where as in urban groups there is significant difference in income levels of SHG members after joining in SHGs. It can be inferred from the results that group enterprises leads to success in urban areas.

Increase in Income – Kerala SHGs

Women were empowered through an increasing control of economic resources, especially income, and

Table 5.29: Percentage Distribution of respondents by increase in income among Andhra Pradesh SHGs

Increase in Income	Andhra Pradesh (Rural) SHGs				Andhra Pradesh (Urban) SHGs			
	Number	Mean	S.D	Paired t' value	Number	Mean	S.D	Paired t' value
Before joining self-help groups	100	1965.00	2435.94	1.682@	100	1853.50	1483.22	4.725*
After joining self-help groups	100	2472.50	1954.65		100	2537.00	1219.3643	

* Significant at 0.05% level; @ Not Significant.

Table 5.30: Percentage Distribution of respondents by increase in income before and after joining in SHGs among Kerala groups

Increase in Income	Kerala (Rural) SHGs				Kerala (Urban) SHGs			
	Number	Mean	S.D	Paired t' value	Number	Mean	S.D	Paired t' value
Before joining self-help groups	100	1831.50	1147.47	4.270*	100	1418.50	81.108	12.115*
After joining self-help groups	100	2214.00	1031.52		100	2157.00	120.58	

* Significant at 0.01% level.

through education. According to a recent study improvement in women's economic position may not only increase their happiness but also enhance their status.

Table 5.30 envisages that there is a significant difference in the levels of income among Kerala SHGs before and after joining the SHGs. The difference is more in urban area. Both in urban groups of Andhra Pradesh and Kerala, SHGs seem to be significantly influencing the income levels of the respondents.

Hence, the null hypothesis, 'that the SHGs had no significant impact on employment generation and increase in income', is rejected.

Economic Motivation

Economic Motivation is an important character that persuades people to adopt improved practices that are proven worthy.

The results in the Table 5.31 reveal that economic motivation differs significantly in case of rural (DWCRA SHGs) and urban (SJSRY-DWCUA) SHGs in Andhra Pradesh. In case of Kerala SHGs, there is no significant difference between rural and urban SHGs.

Table 5.31: Percentage distribution of respondents by economic motivation

Level	Andhra SHGs		χ^2	Kerala SHGs		χ^2
	Rural	Urban		Rural	Urban	
Low	9	35	37.609*	28	28	0.327NS
Medium	65	24		52	55	
High	26	41		20	17	

* Significant at 0.05% level; @ Not Significant.

Sivaprasad (1997) found that economic motivation is an important character that persuades people to adopt improved practices that are proven worthy.

SUM UP

All the women respondents in both the states of Andhra Pradesh and Kerala agreed that self-help groups helped to improve their financial status. With regard to financial self-reliance, SHGs both in Andhra Pradesh and Kerala agreed, that financial decisions were taken by their husbands. Cent per cent of respondents from both the states were of the view that their family living conditions have improved after joining the SHGs. Majority of the respondents in both the states (80% and 100%) had their monthly savings of Rs.50-100 per month. Majority of the respondnets (79%) of Andhra SHGs and Kerala SHGs (82%) stated that there was additional employment generation for more than 200 days per annum had after joining the Self-help groups. Both in urban groups of Andhra Pradesh and Kerala, SHGs were significantly influencing the income levels of the respondents.

A large proportion of Andhra (65% and 24%) and (52% and 55%) Kerala SHGs had medium scores on economic motivation. SHG women who were working for less than 100 days per annum had moved up to higher employment levels. Women who were principally occupied in agriculture prior to DWCRA had shifted to other principal occupations such as dairy, weaving, canteens, readymade units, tailoring and embroidery, handicrafts etc. The occupational shift however was in conformity with their domestic roles. Economic motivation has significantly influenced the members of the SHGs in both the States.

SECTION III

COMPONENTS OF EMPOWERMENT

Empowerment, is a multifaceted process which encompasses many aspects – enhancing awareness, increasing access to resource, mobilisation and organisation of women into groups etc. In the present study, the components of empowerment comprised of issues like achievement motivation, risk taking ability, decision making ability, management orientation, initiativeness and self confidence.

Achievement Motivation

Achievement motivation is the desire to do well, not so much for the sake of the social negotiation or prestige level, but to attain an inner feeling of personal accomplishment.

Table 5.32: Percentage distribution of respondents by achievement motivation

Level	Andhra SHGs		χ^2	Kerala SHGs		χ^2
	Rural	Urban		Rural	Urban	
Low	65	44	20.379*	1	2	6.616*
Medium	32	32		42	25	
High	3	24		57	73	

* Significant at 0.05% level.

A perusal of Table 5.32 makes it clear that of the total SHG members the rural SHG members in Andhra Pradesh had low level of Achievement motivation (65%) while the remaining 32 per cent of both rural and urban SHGs had medium level of achievement motivation. Whereas, the Kerala SHGs members had high levels of achievement motivation both in rural and urban groups i.e., 57 per cent and 73 per cent, 42 per cent of rural and 25 per cent of urban SHG members had medium level of achievement motivation.

Risk-taking Ability

It is defined as the degree to which a rural woman is oriented towards risk and uncertainty and has the courage to face the problems in starting an income generating activity.

Table 5.33: Percentage distribution of respondents by risk taking ability

Level	Andhra SHGs		χ^2	Kerala SHGs		χ^2
	Rural	Urban		Rural	Urban	
Low	52	1	101.246*	43	21	17.545*
Medium	47	44		40	38	
High	1	55		17	41	

* Significant at 0.05% level.

Data presented in Table 5.33 discloses that there is significant difference with regard to risk taking ability among Andhra and Kerala groups. Andhra urban groups had high level of risk taking ability when compared with rural groups. On other hand Kerala urban group had high level of risk taking ability then rural SHGs.

Decision-making ability

Decision making is an important dimension that throws light on the performance of the SHG members. As has been done for achievement motivation, the decision making ability of SHG members in the financial matters has been divided into three categories namely, low, medium and high. From Table 5.34, it may be seen that most of the SHG members belonged to low category of decision-making.

Table 5.34: Percentage distribution of respondents by decision making ability

Level	Andhra SHGs		χ^2	Kerala SHGs		χ^2
	Rural	Urban		Rural	Urban	
Low	52	32	8.210*	69	73	0.389@
Medium	-	-		-	-	
High	48	68		31	27	

* Significant at 0.05% level; @ Not significant.

A glance at the table shows that the level of decision making ability of Andhra groups had significant difference when compared with Kerala SHGs. The urban groups of Andhra had high level of decision making ability than their counterparts. In Kerala the process of arriving at a rational decision was more for urban SHGs of Andhra Pradesh as compared to Kerala SHGs

Management Orientation

Management orientation refers to the degree to which a rural women is oriented towards scientific management comprising of planning, production and marketing in their production unit. The results on management orientation was presented in Table 5.35.

Table 5.35: Percentage distribution of respondents according to their management orientation

Level	Andhra SHGs		χ^2	Kerala SHGs		χ^2
	Rural	Urban		Rural	Urban	
Low	48	70	10.628*	59	52	0.992@
Medium	-	-		-	—	
High	52	29		41	48	

* Significant at 0.05% level; @ Not significant.

There exists a significant difference between Andhra rural and urban self-help groups. Highest score for management orientation is for urban groups. With regard to management orientation among Kerala SHGs, there is significant difference was found between the two groups. Management means getting things done and it is considered as one of the most important factor in making an enterprise profitable. Progress, prosperity and success mainly depends on the managerial role played by women. An individual with high managerial efficiency can effectively utilize the available resources towards achieving the goal. The findings of the study is in conformity with that of Jayalakshmi (1996).

Initiative

It is defined as the capacity of SHG women to come forward on her own to take up some activity.

Table 5.36: Percentage distribution of respondents by initiativeness

Level	Andhra SHGs		χ^2	Kerala SHGs		χ^2
	Rural	Urban		Rural	Urban	
Low	52	38	3.960*	41	52	2.432@
Medium	-	-		-	-	
High	48	62		59	48	

* Significant at 0.05% level; @ Not significant.

A critical review of Table 5.36 shows that 52 per cent of Andhra rural SHGs and 38 per cent of urban SHGs had low level of initiativeness 48 per cent of rural and 62 per cent of urban respondents had high level of initiativeness and the difference was significant. Where as among Kerala SHGs, the difference between rural and urban SHGs was not significant. Majority of rural SHGs (59%) had high level of initiativeness than urban SHGs (48%). High level of aspiration is an indicator of development and this requires free initiation on the part of the respondents only. That is to say that if one has a positive attitude and high level of aspiration naturally the development will be more.

Self-confidence

It refers to the extent of a SHG women about her own powers, abilities and resourcefulness to perform any activity which she desires to undertake.

Table 5.37: Percentage distribution of respondents by self-confidence of SHG members

Level	Andhra SHGs		χ^2	Kerala SHGs		χ^2
	Rural	Urban		Rural	Urban	
Low	21	21	1.242@	55	39	10.314*
Medium	-	-		-	-	
High	66	44		20	42	

* Significant at 0.05% level; @ Not significant.

The results presented in Table 5.37 shows that with regard to self-confidence there is no significant difference between Andhra rural and urban groups where as in Kerala rural groups the difference was highly significant Kerala SHGs had high self-confidence scores because they were venturesome and were dealing with the group. The chances of risk was less and hence had more self-confidence compared to the other groups. Self-confidence is the belief of an individual in his or her own abilities. Participation in the production unit increases the degree of faith among the SHG women by increasing their self-confidence. Hence, the null hypothesis that 'the SHGs had no significant impact on the component of empowerment', is rejected.

SUM UP

Majority of the (65 and 44%) Andhra Pradesh SHG respondents had low level of achievement motivation whereas, majority of the Kerala SHGs (57% and 73%) had high level of achievement motivation. There is significant difference with regard to risk taking ability among Andhra and Kerala Self-help groups. A higher percentage of Andhra Urban SHGs (68%) had higher level of decision making ability than their counterparts. With regard to management orientation among Kerala SHGs significant difference was found between the groups. Nearly half of rural (48%) and urban (62%) Andhra SHGs had high level of initiativeness, 59% and 48% of Kerala rural and urban SHGs had high level of initiativeness. With regard to self-confidence, there is significant difference between rural and urban SHGs of Kerala. Significant differences in components of empowerment was noticed among Andhra Pradesh and Kerala SHGs. The mean difference between rural and urban SHGs was found and the level of significance was beyond 0.1 probability, in comparison with Andhra Pradesh and Kerala SHGs. However it was noted that they are yet to improve and there was a greater need to empower those women integrally. Empowerment manifests itself in improved awareness and Self-confidence, larger roles and responsibilities within the family and in the community, improved self identify and greater participation in decision making. The key objective of Self-help groups is empowerment of women. It is a process of giving power to women to control their own lives.

SECTION IV

EFFECT OF AGE AND EDUCATION ON SOCIO-PSYCHOLOGICAL VARIABLES

Table 5.38, reveals the mean scores, standard deviation and 'F' values of the Andhra SHGs on extension participation, mass media contact, decision making in family and community, credit orientation, attitude towards Self-employment, and perception about self-help groups. Age of the SHG respondents had no significant influence on the socio-psychological variables.

Table 5.38: Effect of age on socio-psychological variables (Andhra SHGs)

S.No.	Variables	Age	Number	Mean	SD	F Value
1.	Extension participation	Young	72	2.097	1.375	0.071@
		Middle	126	2.167	1.349	
		Old	2	2.000	1.414	
2.	Mass media contact	Young	72	2.611	1.623	0.885@
		Middle	126	2.865	2.045	
		Old	2	1.500	0.707	
3.	Decision making in family and community	Young	72	9.167	3.327	0.367@
		Middle	126	8.794	2.852	
		Old	2	8.500	2.121	
4.	Credit orientation	Young	72	13.333	3.373	0.978@
		Middle	126	13.556	3.061	
		Old	2	10.500	3.536	
5.	Attitude towards self-employment	Young	72	28.847	2.771	0.816@
		Middle	126	28.608	3.067	
		Old	2	26.500	0.707	
6.	Perception about SHGs	Young	72	23.944	1.949	1.074@
		Middle	126	24.048	1.987	
		Old	2	26.000	0.000	

@ Not Significant.

It may be inferred from Table 5.39 that the mean scores across the age groups reveals that mass media contact, decision making in family and credit orientation are significant at 5 per cent level. Data on extension participation, attitude towards self-employment and perception about self-help groups revealed the age or the SHG respondents had no significant influence among Kerala groups.

Table 5.39: Effect of age on socio-psychological variables (Kerala SHGs)

S.No.	Variables	Age	Number	Mean	SD	F Value
1.	Extension participation	Young	37	2.595	1.301	0.081@
		Middle	134	2.403	1.383	
		Old	29	2.172	1.167	
2.	Mass media contact	Young	37	3.432	1.608	0.601*
		Middle	134	2.940	1.418	
		Old	29	2.483	1.299	
3.	Decision-making in family and community	Young	37	9.757	3.562	8.865**
		Middle	134	8.873	2.454	
		Old	29	7.034	2.146	
4.	Credit orientation	Young	37	15.514	2.765	7.255**
		Middle	134	15.716	2.250	
		Old	29	13.793	3.028	
5.	Attitude towards self-employment	Young	37	40.865	4.158	0.809@
		Middle	134	39.993	3.894	
		Old	29	39.862	3.553	
6.	Perception about SHGs	Young	37	26.054	3.153	0.756@
		Middle	134	25.963	3.328	
		Old	29	26.759	2.294	

@ Not Significant; * Significant at 0.05% level; ** Significant at 0.01% level

It is evident from Table 5.40 that the mean scores of the age groups do not have any influence on the components of empowerment, no significant difference was found with respect of any dimensions. Age effect on components of empowerment was not found among Andhra Self-help groups.

Table 5.40: Effect of age on components of empowerment (Andhra SHGs)

S.No.	Variables	Age	Number	Mean	SD	F Value
1.	Achievement Motivation	Young	72	18.930	3.681	0.118@
		Middle	126	19.206	3.954	
		Old	2	19.000	0.000	
2.	Management Orientation	Young	72	8.479	1.714	1.336@
		Middle	126	8.667	1.872	
		Old	2	8.000	1.414	
3.	Decision-making ability	Young	72	6.847	2.366	2.325@
		Middle	126	7.262	2.256	
		Old	2	10.000	0.000	
4.	Risk-taking ability	Young	72	19.542	4.179	1.325@
		Middle	126	19.170	3.745	
		Old	2	23.500	0.707	
5.	Initiative	Young	72	5.083	1.143	1.771@
		Middle	126	4.762	1.428	
		Old	2	4.000	0.000	
6.	Self-confidence	Young	72	5.153	1.933	1.187@
		Middle	126	4.833	1.934	
		Old	2	3.500	0.707	

@ Not Significant.

The data in Table 5.41 shows that the impact of age on components of empowerment is not significant as the obtained values in the above table indicates that there is no significant difference with regard to Achievement motivation, management orientation, decision making ability, risk taking ability and self confidence among Kerala SHGs.

Table 5.41: Effect of age on components of empowerment (Kerala SHGs)

S.No.	Variables	Age	Number	Mean	SD	F Value
1.	Achievement Motivation	Young	37	25.081	3.722	0.336@
		Middle	134	24.761	3.215	
		Old	29	23.891	1.896	
2.	Management orientation	Young	37	9.243	1.949	0.336@
		Middle	134	8.948	1.975	
		Old	29	9.034	1.802	
3.	Decision-making ability	Young	37	5.216	2.496	1.375@
		Middle	134	5.754	2.126	
		Old	29	6.069	1.944	
4.	Risk taking ability	Young	37	19.162	5.419	0.578@
		Middle	134	19.493	4.779	
		Old	29	18.448	3.978	
5.	Initiative	Young	37	4.919	1.847	0.682@
		Middle	134	4.993	1.514	
		Old	29	4.862	1.959	
6.	Self-confidence	Young	37	3.486	1.938	0.682@
		Middle	134	3.866	2.095	
		Old	29	4.034	1.973	

@ Not Significant.

In this section the significance of difference between Andhra (Table 5.52) and Kerala (Table 5.53) SHG groups with respect to mean scores is tested by using ANOVA.

The impact of education on socio-psychological variables has been studied with the help of one way analysis of variance. The mean and S.D. along with F-ratio and its significance are presented in Table 5.43.

Table 5.42: Effect of education on socio-psychological Variables (Andhra SHGs)

S.No.	Variables	Age	Number	Mean	SD	F Value
1.	Extension participation	Illiterate	41	1.878	1.327	1.981 @
		Primary	82	2.061	1.211	
		High school	77	2.364	1.486	
2.	Mass media contact	Illiterate	41	2.122	1.005	16.94**
		Primary	82	2.220	1.449	
		High school	77	3.675	2.262	
3.	Decision-making in family and community	Illiterate	41	8.171	2.459	8.347**
		Primary	82	8.305	2.770	
		High school	77	9.987	3.263	
4.	Credit orientation	Illiterate	41	12.878	2.977	0.821@
		Primary	82	13.573	3.348	
		High school	77	13..610	3.104	
5.	Attitude towards self-employment	Illiterate	41	27.780	2.770	4.442*
		Primary	82	28.341	3.060	
		High school	77	29.338	2.799	
6.	Perception about SHGs	Illiterate	41	24.268	1.831	1.151@
		Primary	82	23.780	2.006	
		High school	77	24.169	1.996	

@ Not Significant; * Significant at 0.05% level; ** Significant at 0.01% level.

It is clear from Table 5.42 and Table 5.43 that the mean score across the education is significantly different in Andhra SHGs in the dimensions of mass media contact, decision making in family and community, attitude towards self-employment, whereas among Kerala SHGs significant difference was found only with regard to decision making in family and community, while no difference was observed in other dimensions.

Table 5.43: Effect of education on socio-psychological Variables (Kerala SHGs)

S.No.	Variables	Age	Number	Mean	SD	F Value
1.	Extension participation	Illiterate	8	2.250	1.165	0.056@
		Primary	93	2.409	1.287	
		High school	99	2.414	1.407	
2.	Mass media contact	Illiterate	8	2.500	1.690	2.750@
		Primary	93	2.753	1.349	
		High	99	2.202	1.512	
3.	Decision-making in family and community	Illiterate	8	6.375	2.875	7.608**
		Primary	93	8.290	2.513	
		High school	99	9.414	2.792	
4.	Credit orientation	Illiterate	8	13.875	2.696	5.625@
		Primary	93	14.957	2.541	
		High school	99	15.939	2.440	
5.	Attitude towards self-employment	Illiterate	8	38.625	3.739	1.107@
		Primary	93	39.914	3.964	
		High school	99	40.465	3.834	
6.	Perception about SHGs	Illiterate	8	26.125	2.900	0.256@
		Primary	93	25.925	3.424	
		High school	99	26.253	21.946	

@ Not Significant; * Significant at 0.01% level.

Table 5.44: Effect of education on components of empowerment (Andhra SHGs)

S.No.	Variables	Age	Number	Mean	SD	F Value
1.	Achievement Motivation	Primary	41	17.725	4.750	6.718*
		Middle	82	18.720	3.525	
		High school	77	20.234	3.312	
2.	Management Orientation	Primary	41	8.525	1.961	0.095@
		Middle	82	8.659	1.573	
		High school	77	8.558	1.977	
3.	Decision-making ability	Primary	41	7.561	2.599	1.034@
		Middle	82	6.927	2.287	
		High school	77	7.143	2.156	
4.	Risk-taking ability	Primary	41	17.439	4.410	9.834**
		Middle	82	19.146	3.274	
		High school	77	20.610	3.826	
5.	Initiative	Primary	41	4.756	1.562	0.187@
		Middle	82	4.902	1.384	
		High school	41	4.896	1.154	
6.	Self confidence	Primary	41	4.073	1.385	9.283**
		Middle	82	4.768	1.336	
		High school	77	5.571	2.452	

@ Not Significant; * Significant at 0.05% level; ** Significant at 0.01% level.

The critical review of Table 5.44 shows that the mean scores of education is significantly different in components like achievement motivation, risk taking ability and self-confidence among Andhra SHG members, and in the other dimensions the difference was not significant.

The findings presented in the Table 5.45 indicates that there is no significant difference in all the components of empowerment of the Kerala SHGs.

Table 5.45: Effect of education on components of empowerment (Kerala SHGs)

S.No.	Variables	Age	Number	Mean	SD	F Value
1.	Achievement motivation	Illiterate	8	24.000	2.268	0.213@
		Primary	93	24.763	2.913	
		High school	99	24.687	3.466	
2.	Management Orientation	Illiterate	8	9.500	1.690	2.720@
		Primary	93	8.677	1.872	
		High school	99	9.293	1.986	
3.	Decision-making ability	Illiterate	8	6.625	2.326	0.909@
		Primary	93	5.753	2.348	
		High school	99	5.576	1.995	
4.	Risk-taking ability	Illiterate	8	19.625	5.153	2.787 @
		Primary	93	20.097	4.580	
		High school	99	18.485	4.868	
5.	Initiative	Illiterate	8	5.000	1.307	0.39@
		Primary	93	4.849	1.769	
		High school	99	5.061	1.544	
6.	Self-confidence	Illiterate	8	4.125	2.100	0.722@
		Primary	93	3.978	2.010	
		High school	99	3.646	2.077	

@ Not Significant.

Hence, the null hypothesis that age and education had no significant impact on socio-psychological variables and on components of empowerment, is rejected.

SUM UP

Among Kerala SHGs, age had an effect on socio-psychological variables such as mass media contact, decision making in family and community and credit orientation. The education of the SHGs was significantly influencing the components of empowerment like achievement motivation, risk taking ability and self-confidence. Among both the Andhra Pradesh and Kerala SHGs the obtained mean values indicates that among the SHGs the urban respondents was found to be high than the rural respondents. The Government of India has launched a number of programmes for the promotion of skills, abilities and components among the masses in various spheres. The investigator came to know from the respondents that the literate SHG members were approaching the bankers and government officials directly. Whereas illiterate SHG members were depending on the literates for this purpose.

SECTION V

GROUP VARIABLES

Description of differences in group characteristics and comparison between the States – rural and urban separately is presented in this section.

Group interaction

Group interaction refers to the tendency of members to mix freely with each other without inhibition.

The results presented in Table 5.46 revealed that with regard to group interaction there is a significant difference between Andhra rural self-help groups and Kerala rural self-help groups. The Kerala rural SHGs had high scores in group interaction. Perception of similarity is an important factor that affects group interaction.

Table 5.46: Distribution of respondents according to Group interaction- Rural SHGs

Category	Rural Groups	Mean	SD	t-value
Group Interaction	Andhra SHGs	30.777	1.85	2.8210*
	Kerala SHGs	36.250	5.49	

* Significant at 5% level.

The data in Table 5.47 show that the group interaction among Kerala urban group were very high when compared with Andhra Pradesh urban groups and the difference is also at 5 per cent level of probability. The trend is depicted in Figs. 5.7 and 5.8.

Table 5.47: Distribution of respondents according to Group interaction – Urban SHGs

Category	Urban Groups	Mean	SD	T-value
Group Interaction	Andhra SHGs	32.80	2.4404	3.8900*
	Kerala SHGs	38.42	3.5523	

* Significant at 5% level.

Muller (1997) reported that social participation and training showed positive correlation with group interaction in effective groups.

Group Motivation

Group motivation is defined as the goal directing behaviour of individual members so as to influence mutually in achieving group goals.

Motivation may be external as well as internal for all members. It differs from individual to individual as well as from groups to groups. Kerala rural groups had more score for group motivation and the significant difference is noticed in case of group motivation.

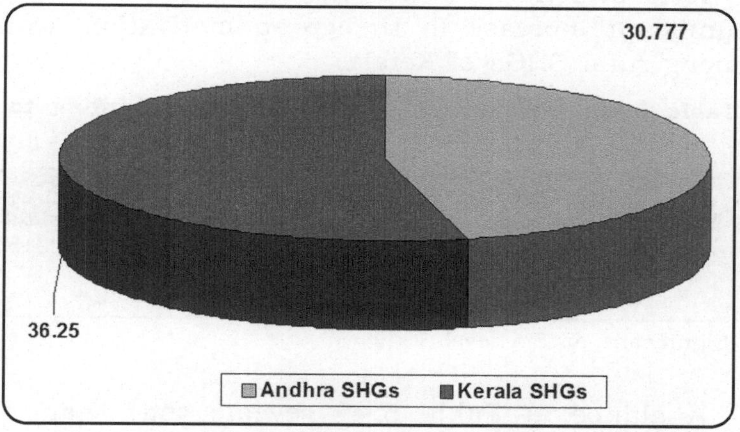

Fig. 5.7: Group Interaction - Rural SHGs

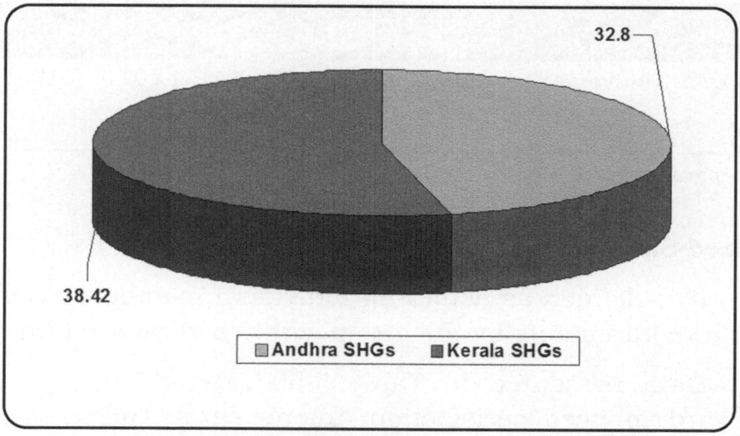

Fig. 5.8: Group Interaction - Urban SHGs

It is evident from the Table 5.48 that there is significant increase in the group motivation score among rural SHGs of Kerala.

Table 5.48: Distribution of respondents according to Group Motivation - Rural SHGs

Category	Rural Groups	Mean	SD	T-value
Group Motivation	Andhra SHGs	21.000	2.7386	7.0313*
	Kerala SHGs	34.3750	4.9262	

* Significant at 5% level.

A glance at Table 5.49 reveals that there is significant difference with regard to group motivation between the two states. Kerala group had a high score as compared to urban Andhra Self-help groups.

Table 5.49: Distribution of respondents according to Group Motivation - Urban SHGs

Category	Urban Groups	Mean	SD	T-value
Group Motivation	Andhra SHGs	24.400	1.8974	5.6148*
	Kerala SHGs	32.285	3.8607	

* Significant at 5% level.

Need-Satisfaction

It is defined as achieving individual members needs and requirements by the group within a stipulated time.

Data presented in Table 5.50 revealed that with regard to need satisfaction among rural Andhra and rural Kerala, rural SHGs of Kerala had high score. As the obtained 't' value was significant beyond 0.05 level or probability, it indicates that there is significant difference between the groups. Need satisfaction is the achievement of individual members needs and requirements over a stipulated period of time.

Table 5.50: Distribution of respondents according to Need satisfaction - Rural SHGs

Category	Rural Groups	Mean	SD	t-value
Group Interaction	Andhra SHGs	30.00	0.000	3.22*
	Kerala SHGs	36.50	6.0710	

* Significant at 5% level.

It is evident from Table 5.51 that the Andhra Pradesh SHGs had high score when compared with Kerala urban SHGs and when the difference was tested, it is significant at 5 per cent level.

Table 5.51: Distribution of respondents according to Need Satisfaction - Urban

Category	Urban Groups	Mean	SD	t-value
Need satisfaction	Andhra SHGs	31.600	1.8379	3.5211*
	Kerala SHGs	38.571	5.9402	

* Significant at 5% level.

Sreedaya (2000) reported that as the people are more experienced and more success oriented they are able to tackle their problems more wisely and try to satisfy their needs.

Equity

Equity refers to how far the group approach minimizes or removes the inequalities in the distribution of inputs, credits, resources and outputs among its members.

Table 5.52: Distribution of respondents according to equity - rural

Category	Rural Groups	Mean	SD	t-value
Equity rural	Andhra SHGs	14.5556	2.0683	6.5975*
	Kerala SHGs	8.8750	1.3562	

* Significant at 5% level.

Hay (1995) Observed that equity means people enjoying equitable access to opportunities. Development without equity means a restriction of choices of many individuals in society. In equity, Andhra rural SHGs mean score was high when compared with Kerala rural SHGs and the difference was significant at 5% level of significance.

Table 5.53: Distribution of respondents according to equity- urban

Category	Urban Groups	Mean	SD	t-value
Equity	Andhra SHGs	11.1000	0.5015	0.6233@
	Kerala SHGs	10.5714		

* Significant at 5% level; @ Not significant.

From Table 5.53, it is evident that there is a no significant difference between the Andhra and Kerala urban SHGs mean scores. Both the groups got the same mean score. Hence the difference between the groups was not significant. Fernandez (1998) reported that for the sustainability of self-help groups, the equity should be ensured.

Group Goal Achievement

It is defined as the extent of the achievement of the group goals by the SHG members of the group.

Table 5.54: Distribution of respondents according to Group goal achievement - Rural

Category	Rural Groups	Mean	SD	T-value
Group goal achievement	Andhra SHGs	27.2	0.44	6.654*
	Kerala SHGs	19.5	3.46	

* Significant at 5% level.

An observation of the above data indicates, an increasing trend of mean scores in Andhra SHGs than Kerala SHGs. The data in the above tables also reveals that the obtained 't' value is significant beyond 0.05 level of probability. It is clear that there is a significant difference in the group goal achievement scores of Andhra Pradesh and Kerala SHGs.

Table 5.55: Distribution of respondents according to group goal achievement - urban

Category	Urban Groups	Mean	SD	t-value
Group goal achievement	Andhra SHGs	27.000	2.7889	3.4493*
	Kerala SHGs	19.8571	5.6988	

* Significant at 5% level.

A cursory glance through the above data reveal that the obtained 't' value (t = 3.449) is significant at 0.05 level of probability. This indicates that Andhra urban SHGs had more group goal achievement than Kerala urban SHGs. Hence, the null hypothesis, is rejected.

Table 5.56: Distribution of respondents according to transparency Rural SHGs

Category	Rural Groups	Mean	SD	T-value
Transparency	Andhra SHGs	15.66	0.00	17.32*
	Kerala SHGs	13.25	6.07	

* Significant at 5% level.

The data show that the difference in the mean scores of transparency between Andhra rural SHGs and Kerala SHGs is significant. The results indicate that Andhra SHG respondents were very transparent in their group activities. Hence the null Hypothesis, is rejected.

O' Brien (1997) is of the opinion that good governance involving participation and transparency were essential for sound development.

Table 5.57: Distribution of respondents according to transparency – Urban SHGs

Category	Urban groups	Mean	SD	T-value
Transparency	Andhra SHGs	15.800	1.6193	1.8475@
	Kerala SHGs	14.5714	0.7868	

@ Not significant.

Mukherjee (1997) reported that some people in community have individualistic approach and do not easily get involved in community efforts. Participatory group approach depends largely on collective activities, initiatives and efforts.

It divulges from Table 5.57 that the obtained 't' value is not significant and that Andhra urban SHGs and Kerala urban SHGs had similar transparency mean scores. That means in both the states urban SHG respondents were not maintaining transparency in group activities.

Interpersonal Communication

Interpersonal communication refers to the communication skill of SHG members which helps them to express their ideas in the group and in turn to know the ideas of the members.

Table 5.58: Distribution of respondents according to Interpersonal communication – Rural

Category	Rural Groups	Mean	SD	t-value
Interpersonal communication	Andhra SHGs	19.1111	1.6159	12.6964*
	Kerala SHGs	34.750	3.2842	

* Significant at 5% level.

Data presented in Table 5.58 revealed that there is a significant difference in interpersonal communication scores between Andhra Rural SHGs and Kerala Rural SHGs. Kerala Rural SHG members had very good interpersonal communication skills than Andhra group, the reason being the higher literacy levels of Kerala women respondents. Hence, the null hypothesis, is rejected.

Table 5.59: Distribution of respondents according to Interpersonal communication - Urban

Category	Urban Groups	Mean	SD	t-value
Interpersonal communication	Andhra SHGs	20.400	3.6576	6.8122*
	Kerala SHGs	32.714	3.6839	

* Significant at 5% level.

The data in Table 5.59 show that there is significant difference with regard to interpersonal communication. The Kerala urban SHGs had higher mean score when compared with Andhra Pradesh urban SHGs. Kerala urban SHGs had good interpersonal communication skills. Hence, the null hypothesis, is rejected.

Group Leadership

It is defined as the role and status of one or more individuals in a group which enables the group to meet the group goals.

Table 5.60: Distribution of respondents according Group leadership - Rural

Category	Rural Groups	Mean	SD	t-value
Group leadership	Andhra SHGs	13.333	1.000	18.03*
	Kerala SHGs	27.625	2.1339	

* Significant at 5% level.

It is clear from Table 5.60 that there is a significant difference between Andhra rural and Kerala rural SHGs about group leadership. Kerala SHGs got higher mean score for group leadership, indicates the Kerala women had more of leadership potential. This variable in turn has relation with the variable interpersonal communication. The more the interpersonal communication the higher the leadership ability. Leadership is the role and status of one or more individuals in a group which enables the group to meet the group goals. Hence, the null hypothesis, is rejected. The trend is depicted in Fig.5.9.

The results presented in Table 5.61 shows that with regard to group leadership there is a significant difference between two groups. Kerala rural groups had high mean score. According to Sitalakshmi and Jyothimani (1994) leadership role played by the group organizer is of great importance in making DWCRA group active. The results are presented in Fig.5.10.

Table 5.61: Distribution of respondents according to group leadership - urban

Category	Urban Groups	Mean	SD	t-value
Group leadership	Andhra SHGs	20.8000	6.2681	3.0036*
	Kerala SHGs	28.8571	3.8914	

* Significant at 5% level.

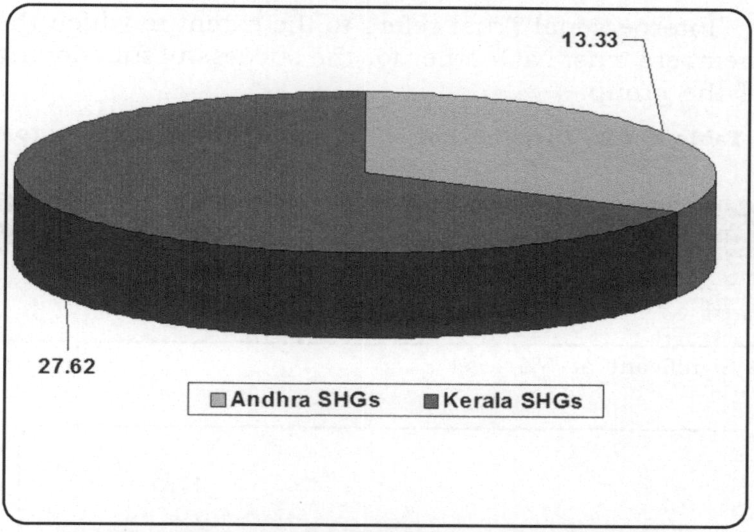

Fig. 5.9: Group Leadership - Rural SHGs

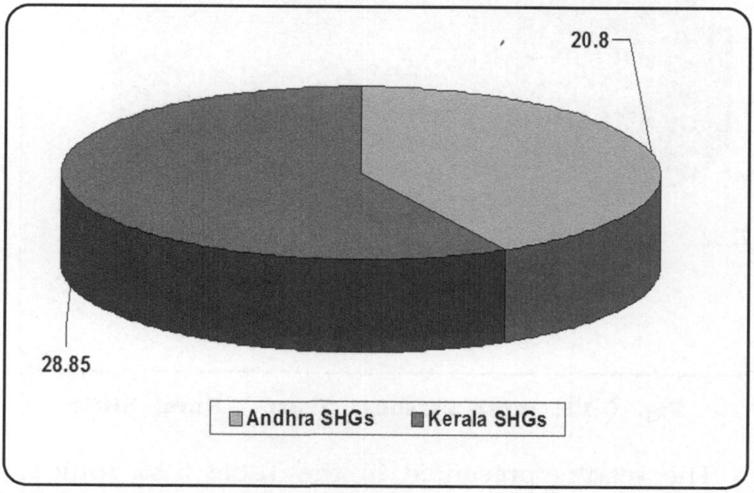

Fig. 5.10: Group Leadership - Rural SHGs

Interpersonal Trust

Interpersonal Trust refers to the extent to which the members trust each other for the successful functioning of the group.

Table 5.62: Distribution of respondents according to interpersonal trust-rural

Category	Rural Groups	Mean	SD	t-value
Interpersonal trust	Andhra SHGs	19.555	2.96	3.274*
	Kerala SHGs	26.625	5.68	

* Significant at 5% level.

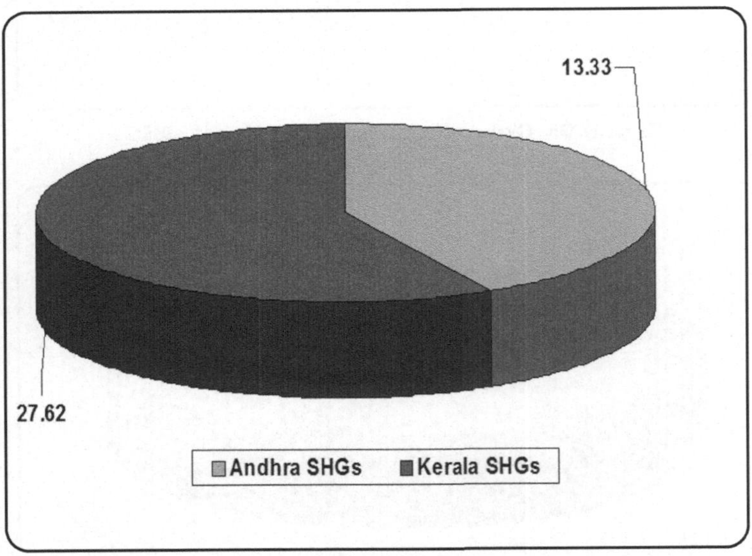

Fig. 5.11: Inter Personal Trust - Rural SHGs

The results presented in the Table 5.62 indicates the mean scores with regard to interpersonal trust of Andhra rural and Kerala rural SHGs. It is clear from the above table that there is a significant difference in the mean scores of interpersonal trust, as the obtained 't' value is significant at 5 per cent level of significance. It is also noticed that some of the members of Kerala groups were relatives and naturally the trust among the group would be more as they knew each other. The results are presented in Fig. 5.11.

Table 5.63: Distribution of respondents according to interpersonal trust - urban

Category	Urban Groups	Mean	SD	t-value
Interpersonal trust	Andhra SHGs	18.5000	3.1358	3.5280*
	Kerala SHGs	25.4286	4.9952	

* Significant at 5% level.

With regard to interpersonal trust, Kerala urban SHGs had a higher mean score as compared to Andhra SHGs and the difference is at 5 per cent level significance. Kerala urban respondents were sharing more interpersonal trust than Andhra urban respondents. Hence, the null hypothesis, is rejected. The results are depicted in Fig. 5.12.

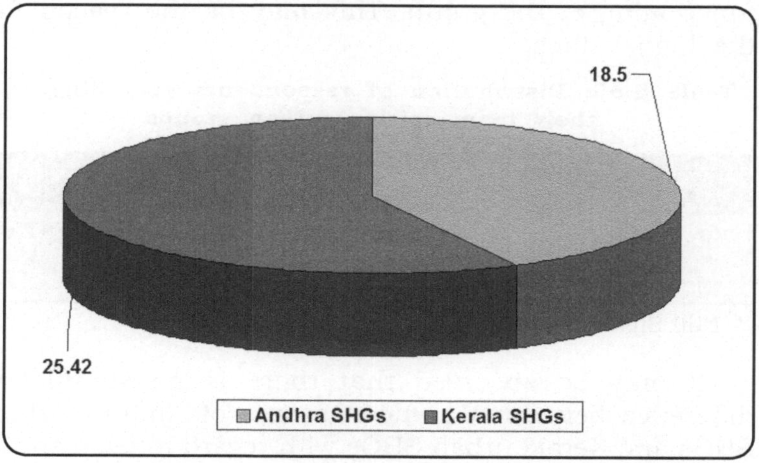

Fig. 5.12: Inter Personal Trust - Urban SHGs

Team Spirit

It refers to the coordinated efforts both physical and mental aspects of the members in order to achieve the best possible results derived by the group.

Table 5.64 : Distribution of respondents according to their team spirit – Rural groups

Category	Rural Groups	Mean	SD	t-value
Team spirit	Andhra SHGs	13.2500	1.7525	3.8145*
	Kerala SHGs	15.667	0.7071	

* Significant at 5% level.

It is evident from the data Kerala rural SHGs had higher team spirit score, when compared with of Andhra Pradesh rural SHGs. The difference between the group is significant at 0.05 level of probability. This is because the members of the rural SHGs of Kerala interact and cooperate with each other during their production activities. The members are mutually dependent with a 'we feeling' and are responsible for the effective functioning of the group. This may be the reason for the high values.

Table 5.65: Distribution of respondents according to their team spirit – urban groups

Category	Urban Groups	Mean	SD	t-value
Team spirit	Andhra SHGs	15.8000	1.6193	1.8475@
	Kerala SHGs	14.5714	0.7868	

@ Not Significant.

It may be observed that there is no significant difference between the mean scores of Andhra urban SHGs and Kerala urban SHGs with regard to team spirit. It is evident that there is an apparent difference between the groups, but the difference is not significant statistically as the calculated 't' value is below the table value even at 0.05 level of probability. That means the urban SHG members in both the states had no team spirit, indicating the influence of urbanization. Hence, the null hypothesis, is retained.

Accountability

Accountability refers to the extent to which members are responsible and answerable for their action or achievement of objectives as decided upon.

The mean values in the above table shows that the Kerala rural SHGs got high mean scores. The findings in the above table signifies a lot of difference in the accountability scores of the Andhra rural and Kerala rural SHGs. The members of Kerala SHGs are mutually dependent with a we feeling and are accountable and responsible to the group. This may be the reason for high group characteristic values.

Table 5.66: Distribution of respondents according to their accountability scores - Rural SHGs

Category	Rural Groups	Mean	SD	t-value
Accountability	Andhra SHGs	6.000	1.1180	7.0342*
	Kerala SHGs	10.5000	1.5119	

* Significant at. 5% level.

Table 5.67: Distribution of respondents according to their Accountability scores - Urban SHGs

Category	Urban Groups	Mean	SD	t-value
Accountability	Andhra SHGs	8.3000	1.595	4.6441*
	Kerala SHGs	11.2857	1.4960	

* Significant at 5% level.

From the Table 5.67, it may be inferred that the Kerala urban SHGs showed higher accountability than Andhra urban SHGs. From the above table, it is clear that the obtained 't' value (t = 4.644) is significant at 5% level of significance, indicating that like Kerala rural SHGS, Kerala Urban SHGs were also having accountability in their group activities than Andhra urban SHGs. Hence, the null hypothesis, is rejected.

The highest group characteristic score of Kerala SHGs may be due to their right choice of group activities with locally available resources, education, interest, mutual understanding, etc. which creates interest in the group members to actively participate in the activities of the group. This in turn will inspire the members to strive for group success and achievement of group goals.

Andhra rural SHGs has the lowest values for the group characteristics namely group interaction, interpersonal trust group motivation, interpersonal communication, team spirit, equity and Kerala rural SHGs had the lowest values for equity and accountability.

The group characteristic values of Andhra urban SHGs has the lowest values for group interaction, interpersonal trust, group motivation, group goal achievement, group leadership, need satisfaction etc. and the Kerala urban SHGs has the lowest values for team spirit, equity and accountability.

The poor group characteristic values of these groups may be due to lack of interest, wrong choice of group activity or poor leadership.

SUM UP

Of the group variables, a highly significant difference was found between Andhra Pradesh and Kerala SHGs in group interaction, group motivation, Need satisfaction, group goal achievement, interpersonal communication, group leadership, interpersonal trust and accountability.

It is noticed that majority of the Kerala rural and urban SHGs got high mean score for group interaction. It is noticed that the members of Kerala group freely mix with each other and this may be the reason for the high group score. With regard to group motivation, need satisfaction, interpersonal communication, group leadership, interpersonal trust and accountability Kerala SHGs had higher mean scores. It may be concluded that group action efforts Kerala SHGs had created tremendous impact on the respondents to have better group characteristics score.

The figure shows the significant relationship of socio-psychological, economic and group characteristics of the SHG respondents in Andhra Pradesh and Kerala. The socio-psychological variables like extension participation, mass media contact, attitude towards self-employment decision making in family and community and self-esteem had significant relationship among Andhra Pradesh rural and urban SHGs.

With regard to the empowerment components viz., increase in income economic motivation, achievement motivation, risk-taking ability, decision making ability, initiativeness and self-confidence figured significant relationship in both Andhra Pradesh rural & urban SHGs and also among Kerala rural and urban SHGs. Among Kerala SHGs age had an effect on variables like mass media contact, decision making in family and community. Among both the Andhra Pradesh and Kerala SHGs the obtain mean values indicate that among the SHGs urban respondents was found we high then the rural respondents. The group variables like group interaction, group motivation, need satisfaction,

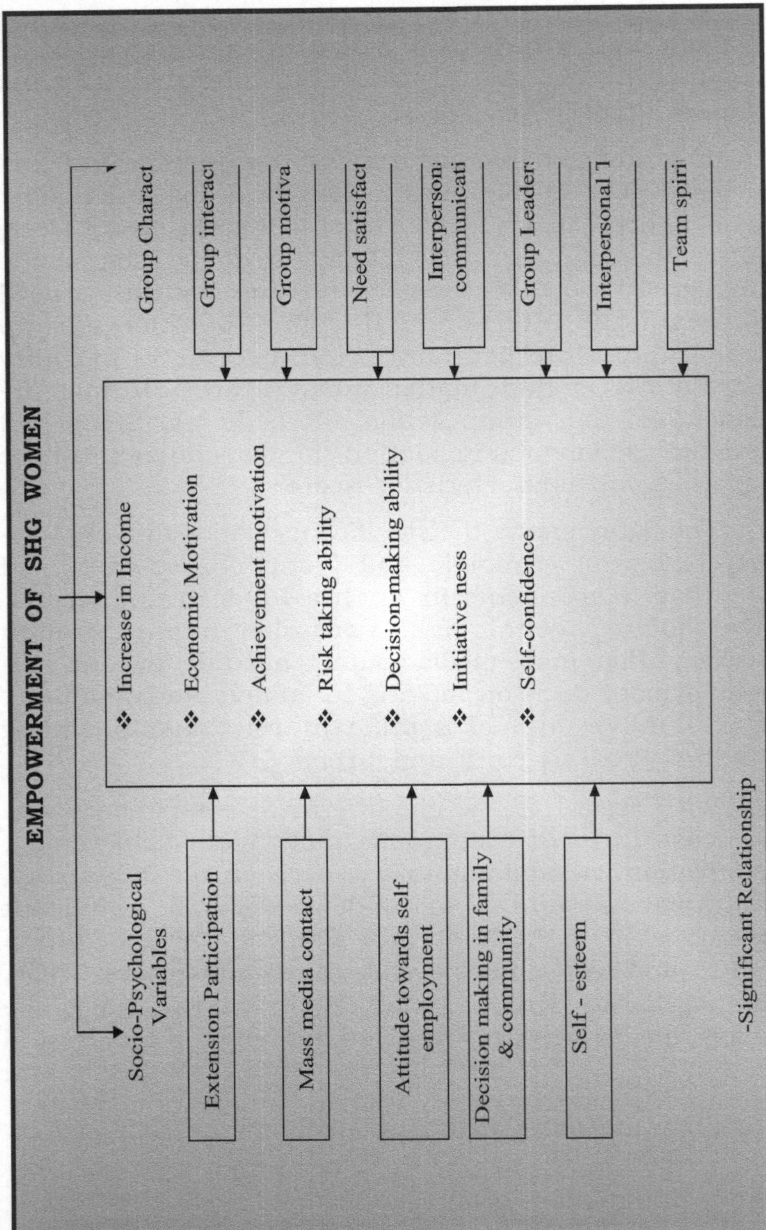
EMPOWERMENT OF SHG WOMEN
Socio-Psychological Variables
Extension Participation
Mass media contact
Attitude towards self employment
Decision making in family & community
Self - esteem
Increase in Income
Economic Motivation
Achievement motivation
Risk taking ability
Decision-making ability
Initiative ness
Self-confidence
Group Charact
Group interact
Group motiva
Need satisfact
Interperson communicati
Group Leader
Interpersonal T
Team spiri
-Significant Relationship

group goal achievement, interpersonal communication, interpersonal trust and team spirit figured significant influence on both rural and urban SHGs among Andhra self-help groups.

The group characteristics like group interaction, group motivation, need satisfaction, group goal achievement, interpersonal communication, group leadership, interpersonal trust, and team spirit shows significant influence on both rural and urban SHGs.

CHAPTER 6

SUMMARY AND CONCLUSIONS

INTRODUCTION

Women constitute half of the population and contributing substantially for the socio-economic development of the families and the nation as a whole. However, this contribution was recognized in domestic spheres and not accounted in terms of economy. Most women in India are dependent on land based livelihood than men. Yet they have less access to landownership and other property, credit facilities, income generating programmes and live in abject poverty. The concept of human poverty has been well defined by Dr. Amartya Sen as a kind of economic insufficiency, as an absence of certain capabilities and skills, as a political and economic exclusion. For the empowerment of women in every field, economic independence is of paramount importance.

The emergence of micro-credit system is an alternative system and is generally recognized as a powerful tool for empowering women. To bridge the gap between demand and supply of funds in the lower rings of the rural economy, the formal sector took the initiative to develop a supplementary credit delivery mechanism by encouraging institutional arrangements outside the financial system. Micro-credit is distinctly different from other populist poverty alleviation schemes. This is a concept of economic empowerment of women through the formation and nurturing of Self-help Groups (SHGs) of the target population.

Micro-credit and Micro-finance is emerging as a powerful instrument for poverty alleviation in the new economy. In India, micro-finance scene is dominated by SHG-Bank Linkage programme aimed at providing a cost effective mechanism for providing financial services to the 'Unreached Poor'. The SHG programme has been successful in not only meeting peculiar needs of the rural poor, but also in strengthening collective self-help capacities of the poor at the local level leading to their empowerment.

Empowerment is a process of change by which individuals or groups gain power and ability to take control over their lives. It involves increased well-being, access to resources increased self-confidence, self-esteem and respect, increased participation in decision making and increased control over benefits, resources and own life. Micro-credit or micro-finance for the poor women has received extensive recognition as a strategy for poverty reduction and for economic empowerment. In a country like India, economic uncertainties, loss of livelihood, inflation, lack of access to natural resources, natural disaster etc make the poor extremely vulnerable. In this context, it would be necessary to ensure that the poor are empowered to access development resources and use it to their greatest benefit.

JUSTIFICATION OF THE STUDY

In India, even today in certain regions and states majority of the women are plagued by illiteracy, poverty and lack of basic amenities in addition to the major responsibility of maintaining the family. This necessitated the effort to identify and take up various incomes generating activities to supplement the family's income which resulted in the formation of a large number of self-help groups in India. As such India has become one of the countries where SHGs and micro-enterprise play an effective role in women's development.

Micro-credit programme through self-help groups is different from poverty alleviation programmes. It targets the rural and urban households below the poverty line and assures the poor women of employment and income. Micro credit savings helps the women to come out of the clutches of the moneylenders. Further, savings can also be ploughed back into the common fund. Micro credit through self-help groups helps the poor women to build their skills and capacities and provide access to finances without any collateral and empowers them not only economically, but also socially.

Self-Help Group in short, is a sustainable organizational setup which disburses micro-credit to the poor women and encourages them to enter into entrepreneurial activities. Women lead self-help groups in many parts of our country have achieved success in bringing them to the mainstream of decision making. Self-help groups serve as a source of inspiration and a viable alternative for achieving the objective of socio-economic development for women by involving them in all development programmes.

In Andhra Pradesh, there are about 6.5 lakhs of SHGs functioning in the state formed by DRDA under the Indirakranthi Padam (IKP) programme. All the districts in Andhra Pradesh are covered by SHG bank linkage programme and Chittoor is one of the leading districts among them. The SHGs are also popularly called IKP groups. The study district has a record number of 50,000 SHGs, which figure significantly in a big way in aleviating poverty and empowering women. Similarly the State of Kerala also has made significant strides in the field of micro finance. The success of Kudumbasree and the wide publicity of SHG strategy have attracted several other agencies. Formal agencies like District Collectorate, Primary Agricultural Credit Societies, Department of Industries, Development of Agriculture and various other government agencies are how actively promoting SHGs in Kerala for the effective utilization of their funds.

The role of NABARD in the growth of SHGs in Kerala is worth mentioning. Kerala remains the third largest in the country next only to Karnataka and Andhra Pradesh in the matter of the number of linked groups and accounted for 13 per cent of the total linked groups in India in 1999 (Kerala Status focus paper, NABARD 2000). The number of self-help groups increased from 352 in 1994-95 to 2434 in 1999-2000, recording a growth of around seven times over a period of five years. The highest number of groups was in Alappuzha district (996) and the amount of bank loan distributed was also the highest in the district (Rs.131.09 lakh).

In our country, during the past five decades efforts have been made to improve the status of women by various strategies and through development programmes. The neglect of women in the development process and the immediate need for appropriate attention on women to enable to attain requisition position has been emphasized. The States of Andhra Pradesh and Kerala witness gigantic strides in terms of women empowerment through micro credit. However all SHGs are not equally successful. Therefore, research on factors which are figuring in the success of SHGs would facilitate the unsuccessful SHGs in their economic ventures. Research studies penetrating into these aspects are always essential to understand the process of SHG movement in a much better way for realizing the potential and benefits of Self-Help Group movement.

However, all Self-help Groups have not successfully contributed to the upliftment of the poor women. Therefore, in order to find out what are the factors contributing to the success of self-help groups, the present research study was undertaken.

OBJECTIVES OF THE STUDY

The general objective of the study was:

To examine the self-help group and its beneficiaries in Andhra Pradesh and Kerala and identify the factors contributing to success and failure of the self-help groups.

The specific objectives of the study were:

- To study the socio-demographic and psychological profile of SHG women beneficiaries in the States of Andhra Pradesh and Kerala.
- To asses the level of participation of Self-Help Groups women in decision making at family and community in Andhra Pradesh and Kerala.
- To examine the impact of programme on employment generation of self-help group women in Andhra Pradesh and Kerala.
- To assess the improvement in the economic status of women in Andhra Pradesh and Kerala before and after joining self-help group.
- To compare and analyze the components of empowerment in the status of Andhra Pradesh and Kerala, and
- To analyze the group characteristics of SHG women beneficiaries in Andhra Pradesh and Kerala.

HYPOTHESES

Based on the above objectives, the following hypotheses are formulated:

- v There is no significant difference in the socio-demographic and psychological characteristics of SHG women beneficiaries in Andhra Pradesh and Kerala.
- v Differences in the levels of participation of SHG women of Andhra Pradesh and Kerala had no significant effect on the decision making capacity at family and community level.
- v There is no significant improvement in the economic status of SHG women beneficiaries in Andhra Pradesh and Kerala after joining SHG programme.
- v There is no significant variation in the components of empowerment of SHG women beneficiaries in Andhra Pradesh and Kerala and
- v There is no significant difference in the group characteristics of SHG women beneficiaries in Andhra Pradesh and Kerala.

VARIABLES USED

The independent variables included in the present study were age, religion, caste, educational status, marital status, type of house, type of famly, family size, landholding, occupation of husbands, annual income etc. and the socio-psychological aspects include training, social participation, extension participation, mass-media contact, attitude towards self-employment, decision making in family and community, perception about SHGs, Self-esteem, Cosmopoliteness. The dependent variables included in the study were Achievement motivation, risk taking ability, management orientation, Decision making ability, Initiativeness and Self-confidence and the group variables namely, group interaction, group motivation, need satisfaction, equity, and group goal achievement.

TOOLS USED

To find out the variations among the SHG beneficiaries in both the States, three schedules were prepared consisting of three parts, namely, demographic and socio-psychological variables. Economic empowerments and components of empowerment and group characteristics of Self-Help Groups.

LOCALE OF THE STUDY

The locale of the study was the state of Andhra Pradesh and Kerala in India. The districts selected were Chittoor district in Andhra Pradesh and Palakkad district in Kerala. In Andhra Pradesh., Madanapalle urban and Kothapalle rural Panchayat were selected. Similarly in Kerala Ottapalam urban and Ambalapara rural Panchayat of Palghat district, were selected.

SAMPLE SELECTED

The study covered a total sample of 400 SHG beneficiaries from both the states. The SHGs of DWCRA and DWCUA groups from both urban and rural panchayats i.e., 200 SHG members from Andhra Pradesh and 200 SHG members from Kerala were selected.

COLLECTION OF DATA

To collect the data, interview schedules were used, which covered demographic, socio-psychological, economic and group variables. They were pre-tested on 50 respondents outside the study area. After analyzing each item based on the pre-test results and field experience, the schedules have been finalized. The schedules were administered personally to all the 400 respondents and the responses of the SHG beneficiaries were scored for the purpose of analysis.

SCORING AND ANALYSIS

The schedules were scored by assigning the appropriate weightages to obtain numerical values on the various variables measured. The total scores obtained by each of the 400 respondents on all the variables were computed. The data were carefully analyzed by employing appropriate statistical techniques like chi-square, 't' test and 'F' ratio, to know whether the independent variables could influence significantly the dependent variables. The salient findings of the study were presented below.

MAJOR FINDINGS OF THE PRESENT STUDY

A high percentage (67% and 59%) or the rural and urban SHG of Andhra Pradesh (71% and 63%) of Kerala Self Help groups belonged to the age group of 31-50 years.

A large proportion (94% and 78%) rural and urban SHGs of Andhra Pradesh, (93% & 91%) of Kerala rural and urban SHGs belongs to Hindu religion.

A majority of the (79% & 63%) of rural and urban SHGs of Andhra Pradesh and (49% and 64%) of Kerala SHGs belonged to backward castes.

Nearly one-fourth (22%) of rural SHGs and (55%) of urban SHGs of Andhra Pradesh had education above high school level among Kerala SHGs more than half of the rural SHGs (57%) and (42%) of urban SHGs had education above high school level.

A high proportion (93% and 74%) of Andhra rural and urban SHGs and (76%) of rural and urban SHGs respondents of Kerala were married.

Nearly three-fourths (74%) of rural SHGs and (43%) of urban SHGs of Andhra Pradesh (82% and 59%) of Kerala SHGs were living in tiled houses.

More than half (64% and 70%) of rural and urban SHGs of Andhra Pradesh, more than three fourths (80% and 83%) of Kerala rural and urban SHGs belonged to nuclear families.

More than half (54% and 58%) of rural and urban SHGs of Andhra Pradesh (62% and 70%) of Kerala SHGs had less than four members in their family.

A greater proportion of respondents (93% and 67%) of rural and urban SHGs of Andhra Pradesh (66% and 76%) of rural and urban SHGs of Kerala owned less than 5 cents of land.

More than half (53%) of rural SHGs of Andhra Pradesh were non-agricultural labourers and 46% of urban SHGs were engaged in business and other activities while among Kerala SHGs (42%) of rural SHGs were engaged in farming and (49%) of urban SHGs were non-agricultural labourers.

Higher proportion (81% and 80%) of rural and urban SHGs of Andhra Pradesh (70% and 78%) of Kerala rural and urban SHGs members had an annual income of rupees 10,000-25,000 per annum.

Nearly half (46%) of rural SHGs and (80%) of urban SHGs of Andhra Pradesh attended three or more training programmes (55%) of rural SHGs (70%) of urban SHGs of Kerala attended three or more training programmes.

Almost cent percent (99% and 100%) of rural and urban SHGs of Andhra Pradesh and (91% and 96%) of Kerala SHGs were members of one organization.

Of the socio-psychological variables there is significant difference between rural and urban SHGs, of Andhra Pradesh with the dimensions, extension participation, mass media contact, attitude towards self-employment, decision making in family and community and self esteem. While among Kerala rural and urban SHGs the significant difference was found for the dimensions extension participation and mass media contact.

With regard to economic empowerment cent per cent of respondents in both the States of Andhra Pradesh and Kerala opined that there is an increase in women earning capacity and improvement in financial status of the family after joining Self-help groups.

Kerala self-help groups had significant difference with the components of empowerment like achievement motivation, risk taking ability and self-confidence.

Age have significant influence on mass media contact, decision making in family and community and credit orientation among Kerala self-help groups.

Education have an impact on variables like mass media contact, decision-making in family and community and attitude towards self-employment among Andhra SHGs and among Kerala SHGs significant difference was found with regard to decision making in family and community.

Regarding the effect of education on components of empowerment Andhra SHGs have significant difference in components such as achievement-motivation, risk-taking ability and self confidence.

Of the group variables, the variables such as group interaction, group motivation, need satisfaction, equity, group goal achievement, interpersonal communication, group leadership, interpersonal trust, team spirit and accountability signifies a lot of difference among rural SHGs of Andhra Pradesh and Kerala.

Almost all the respondents in both the States expressed that their family living conditions have improved after joining the SHGs.

Cent per cent of the respondents in both the states have their monthly savings of Rs. 50 to 100.

More than three fourths (79%) of Andhra Pradesh SHGs had an employment generation of above 200 days per annum and (82%) of Kerala SHGs had an employment generation for more than 200 days per annum.

Among urban SHGs of Andhra Pradesh there is significant difference in income levels of SHG members before and after joining in Self help groups.

With regard to increase in income Kerala rural and urban SHGs shows significant difference in the levels of income before and after joining self-help groups.

Economic motivation differs significantly in case of rural and urban self-help groups of Andhra Pradesh.

The components of empowerment like, achievement motivation, risk taking ability, decision-making ability, management orientation and initiativeness had significant difference between rural and urban SHGs of Andhra Pradesh.

A comparative analysis of the group variables among urban SHGs of Andhra Pradesh and Kerala indicates that there was significant difference in the variables like group interaction, group motivation, need satisfaction, group goal achievement, transparency, interpersonal communication, group leadership, interpersonal trust and accountability.

IMPLICATIONS OF THE STUDY

In order to make self-help groups economically viable and more functional in nature and to integrate women into the mainstream of development rather than isolating their activities. Following are a few implications to improve the performance of the self-help group members.

Most of the members of self-help groups are illiterate. Hence, they should be given education by establishing non-formal education centres in each area both for providing basic education as well as continuing of education.

Periodical time-to-time learning by giving training for updating the knowledge of the self-help groups for sharpening their skills, and for creating a right positive attitude in them, make them inventors and early adopters would be a great helping resource.

The training programmes and meetings should be conducted at the residential areas of the members in which there is every possibility of women to attend it.

Training should be supported by extension service and adequate supply of inputs, even after the completion of the training, and the training institution should maintain close contacts with the trainees in order to assess their performance or ascertain their problems, if any.

Government should give special training to self help group members in handicrafts. This type of training may help them to improve their quality of products and also improve their standard of living.

Government officials should cooperate with group leaders and members for successful implementation of the schemes.

Some of the SHG beneficiaries had no clear idea about thrift and loans. They have to be educated and awareness has to be created with regard to the process of these schemes.

Awareness programmes are to be conducted to the members regarding health, education and environmental conditions.

Efforts should be putforth by the group to ensure consistent and compatible quality of the products manufactured by them.

The amount sanctioned under the scheme is often inadequate for economic viability of the group. Therefore, it should be raised to a viable level.

Transport facilities should be provided to self-help groups women for marketing their products.

The gross root level officials responsible for the implementation of the programme should be given incentives to motivate the groups for better performance.

It should be made mandatory for the government institution to purchase the required items from self-help groups only, subject to their availability. This would solve the market problems to a great extent.

To encourage SHG women, NGOs must help them start new business ventures like photo lamination, paper machine, sericulture, basket weaving, etc.

Giving them orientation, induction training and acquaint them with the objectives and some of the principles of working in groups and in community would go a long way for their success.

Rural female work force is a heterogeneous group. Some of the group have hidden potential and skills. Hence, while women were brought under certain target groups, traditional skills are to be located and, if possible programmes are to be undertaken to enhance their skills and to take-up programmes accordingly.

The selected target group should be brought under achievement motivation training in order to make the self employment programmes more effective and enduring.

A sense of entrepreneurship and profit motivation as well as an attitude of cosmopolitans and venture some ness should be developed in them.

Educational institutions should be given responsibility for implementing and monitoring the self-help groups successfully.

The existing skills need to be upgraded and new skills related to their respective areas of production and marketing should be imparted. Women should undergo some vocational training to utilize the money properly.

Their should be regular monitoring and effective follow up of the unit.

SUGGESTIONS FOR FURTHER STUDY

A comparative study can be undertaken on samples of schedule castes and schedule tribes of similar education and economic background.

More sample could be covered so that accurate generalizations could be drawn.

Similar study may be undertaken on women empowerment through NGO interventions.

A comparative investigation can be undertaken to know the life styles of SHG beneficiaries before and after joining in the self-help groups.

BIBLIOGRAPHY

Agarwal, D. (2001): Empowerment of rural women in India, *Social Welfare*, Vol.48, No.4.

Alex, P. Jiju, (1994): Role of Agricultural labourers in decision making in paddy production by farmers in Thiruvanthapuram district, M.Sc. (Ag.) thesis, K.A.U, Thrissur.

Anand, U.K. (2001): Micro-credit – A venue for sustainable empowerment of rural women, *Social Welfare*, Vol.48, No.4.

Anne, M.H. and King. M.E. (1995): Women education and Economic well being, *Feminist Economics*, Vol.1, No.2, London.

Anonymous, (1996): *Financing Self-help groups "Swayam-Seva"*, Indian Bank, Central Office, Madras.

Anonymous, (1999): Swarozgaris Towards self reliance, *Kurukshethra*, 4(2) 1-4.

Appa Rao (2002): Group farming as a basis for efficient resource utilization for small and marginal farmers - *Regional workshop on group farming*, NIRD, Hyderabad.

Bandya Padhyaya, D. (2000): Gender and governance in India" *Economic and Political Weekly*, July 29, 2000.

Bardhan, (1993): Analysis of the institutions of informal cooperation in rural development, *World Development*, 21 (4).

Basu, et al., (2002): Empowerment of women in the context of development: Some issues and suggestions, *Journal of the Indian Anthropological Society*, 37(3), 209-221. November,

Beebington, A.J. (1991): Farmer organization in Ecuador-contribution to farmer first research and development, *Gatekeeper Series No.26*, IIEP, London.

Beyson, (1997): Folk believes associated with dry farming, *Indian Journal of Extension*, 16(3): 4.

Boserup, Esther (1990): *Women's Role in Economic Development*, New York, St. Martins Press.

Cambessus, M (1998): Boldly reform development, Department of International Development (DFID), London, Issue No.4: 26-27.

Chartterjee, S. (2004): Empowering women through microfinance, *Women's Link*, Vol. 10, No. 3-15.

Choudhary (1997): *New partnership in rural development*, Himalayan Publishers, New Delhi, p.35-93.

Choudhary Anand Meenaxi (1996) : Empowering strategies for rural women in India. *Kurukshetra*, 1996.

Clark Amer (2001): *Community mobilization for SHG formation and economic activation*. International institute of development management technology, International programme, Jaipur, India.

Dangwal R.C. (2000): *Development of women Entrepreneurship in South Asian Region*, edited by Kalpana Sinha, AMDISA, Hyderabad.

Dhulari Birundha (2000): *Women and their interaction in sustainable development, women and economic development*, Deep and Deep Publications, pp.73-78.

Dodkey, M.D. (1998): SHGs and Micro credit-sustaining Rural Women, *Social Welfare*: 45(12).

Dwaraki, B.R. Narayana Swamy, N. Ramesh, N. (1996): Towards creating a participatory Self-help credit co-operative - rediscovering cooperation, Indian Institute of Rural Management, Anand, Gujarat, pp.216-235.

Edward, E.W. and Hulne, V.N (1994): Indigenous organizations development the case of irrigation, *Journal of Development Studies.*

Emancipation through Participation: Study of Women Groups in Andhra Pradesh. Website of Commissioner of Women Empowerment, Government of Andhra Pradesh, Hyderabad.

FAO (1999) : Proceedings of the FAO E-mail conference on small farmer group association bringing the poor together. 24 September – 11 November, 1998 FAO of UN Rural Institution and participation services, Rome.

Fernandez, A.P (1998): Self-help groups in watershed management, ILEIA Newsletter 14(1): 12-13.

Fernando, S. (1995): *Theory and practice of participatory development at grass-root level: Fact and Nation in Srilanka in Readmit Schneider*, Participatory development from advocacy to action.

Friedmann, J. (1992): *The Empowerment: The Politics of Alternative Development*, Oxford Bachelor.

Gangadharan (1993): Adoption of improved agricultural practice by pepper growers of Idukki District, M.Sc. (Ag.) thesis, K.A.U. Thrissur.

Garforth, C. (1993): Rural peoples organization and Agricultural Extension in the Upper north of Thailand: who benefits, University of Reading, Mimeo.

Geetha, T.K. (1998): *Haritha Pachakari Krishi Samrithiyilekku, Kerala Karshakam*, p.15.

Ghosh, D.K. (1995): Group cohesiveness in DWCRA groups – an application of socio-metric approach, *Kurukshethra*, XLIII, 67-70.

Goutham, N Singh (1990) : Development of women and children in rural areas. An appraisal, *Kurukshetra*, 39 (33) : 45-47.

Government of India (1997-2002) : Ninth Five-year Plan. The World Bank (2000-01) World Development Report, p.114.

Government of India (2001): Guidelines, Swarnajayanthi Gram Swarozgar Yojana, Ministry of Rural Development, New Delhi.

Gupta, A. Das (1999): Rural Banking for women, *Social Welfare*: 65(12).

Gupta, S.K (2002): Formation and functioning of SHGs in Hoshangabad district of Madhya Pradesh, *Land Bank Journal*, 41(1), 25-31, June.

Gurumoorthy, T.R. (2000): Self-help groups empower rural women, *Kurukshethra*, 25(8).

Hansari, B.S. (1998): Agricultural transfer of technology approaches since independence in India, *Journal of Extension Education* 9 (4): pp.2168-2174.

Harikumar, S. (1990): Group farming in paddy cultivation – An emerging trend in Kerala. *Indian Journal of Agricultural Economics*. 45(3): 237-238.

Rao, H.C. (1995): DWCRA – A means of women's empowerment – case study of a DWCRA group - *Rural Development Trust* p.35-40.

Hashemi, S.M. (1996): Rural credit programmes and women empowerment in Bangladesh, *World Development*, Vol.24, No.4, pp.635-653.

Hay, M. (1995): *Reflections of Human Development*, Oxford University Press, Newyork.

Hussain, M.M. (1992): Group management in rice production – An action research, Ph.D thesis, K.A.U, Thrissur.

Hussain, S (1998): "*Adayaman Harithayude Vijayagatha*", *Kerala Karshakam*, p.14.

Indira Kumari, Y. and Sambasiva Rao, B. (2005): *Empowerment of women and Rural Development*, Serials Publications, New Delhi.

Indrabhushan Singh and Usha Kumari (2007): Rural development and women Empowerment, *Kurukshetra*, Vol. 55, No.5, pp.3-8.

Institute of social and economic change (2002): Microfinance, poverty alleviation and empowerment of women: A study of two NGOs from Andhra Pradesh and Karnataka, *Agricultural Situation in India*, 59(7), 435-37, October.

Jairam Ramesh (2007): Selfhelp group Revolution: What Next? *Economic and Political Weekly*, Vol. XLII No.36, P.3621-3623.

Jaya and Anand, (1999): Impact of the micro credit problems on empowering women, *Journal of Institute for Management in Government*, Tiruvananthapuram.

Jayalakshmi, G. (2001): Empowerment of rural women through self-help groups - An action research, Ph.D. (Ag.) thesis, KAU, Thrissur.

Jayalakshmi, K. (2000): Rural women's development: Corporation vis-a-vis local institutions in Karnataka, *Women's Link*, 6(2), 19-23, April.

Jayalekshmi, G. (1996): Entrepreneurial behaviour of rural women in Trivandrum District, M.Sc., (Ag.) thesis TNAU, Coimbatore.

Jha P.N, (2004): Self-help groups in accelerating transfer of technology for promoting sustainable agriculture and entrepreneurship development, *Journal of Indian Farming.*

Jhingam, M.L (1990): *Micro economic theory*, Konark Publishers, Pvt. Ltd., New Delhi, p.266-271.

John, T.D., (1991): Feasibility Analysis of group approach in transfer of pepper production technology, M.Sc. (Ag.) thesis, K.A.U. Thrissur.

Jyothy (2002): Self-help groups under the women's development programmes in Tamil Nadu: Achievements, Bottlenecks and recommendations. *Social Change*, 32 (3 & 4), 195-204, September – December.

Kafmakar *et. al.*, (2002): Role of women in the SHG: An emerging possibility to co-operavization at grass-root, *Men in India*, 82(3 & 4), 441-451, July-December.

Kamarudeen, M. (1981): A study on the impact of National Demonstration on paddy cultivation in Thrissur District, M.Sc. (Ag.) Thesis. KAU, Thrissur.

Kantor, Paula (2003): Women's empowerment through home based work: Evidence from India, *Development and Change*, 34(3), 425-445, June.

Karmakar, K.G. (1998): Self-help groups in Orissa-some conceptual issues, *Prajnan* 26(2), 123-131.

Kaur, Dil Bagh *et. al.*, (2002): Rural Women entrepreneurs: A study in Rural Tamil Nadu, Abhigyan, 20(4), 27-31, January – March.

Kerlinger, F.N (1973): *Foundations of Behavioural Research*, Holt, Rinehart and Winston, New York.

Krishnamurthy, G. (1996): Self-help organization – A case study of thrift and credit co-operatives of Adilabad district, Andhra Pradesh – rediscovering cooperation, Indian Institute of Rural management, Anand, Gujarat, 2.263.

Kumaran, K.P. (1997): SHGs and alternative to institutional credit to the poor- A case study in Andhra Pradesh, *Journal of Centre for Social Development*, Vol.14, No.1.

Kumud Sharma (1994) : Gender Environment and Structured Adjustment, *Economic and Political Weekly*, April, 30.

Lalitha, N. and Nagarajan, B.S. (2000): *Self-help groups in rural development.*

Laxmi, R. Archana Gupta (2001): Self-help groups innovations in financing the poor, *Kurukshethra*, Vol.4, 26-29.

Leelamma Devasia and Jancy Antony. (2004): Social development issues in Self-help groups, *Social Welfare*, Vol.5, No.10.

Likert, Rensis (1961): *New Patterns of management*, Mc Graw-Hill Co, New York, pp.113-115.

Manimekalai, N. (1999): Rural women beneficiaries of DWCRA scheme, *Kurukshethra*, Vol.47, No.9, p.3-6.

Medha Dhubhasi (2004): Expert committee on rural credit – findings and Recommendations, *Kurukshetra*, pp.29-31.

Meera, M.J. (2001): Performance of Samatha Self-help groups in the empowerment of rural women in Ulloor Panchayat, M.Sc. (Ag.) thesis, KAU, Thrissur.

Mishra J.C. and Thanvi, R.K. (2004): Indian Banking system and Micro-finance. *Kurukshethra*, Feb.2004, pp.12-15.

Mishra, S.K. and Puri, V.K. (2000): *Poverty Alleviation Programmes in India, Indian Economy*, Himalaya Publishing House, Delhi.

Mishra, S.N. and Mishra, S. (1998): Good governancy, *Indian Journal of Public Administration*, Vol.24, No.3, New Delhi.

Mukherjee, N. (1997): *Participatory appraisal of natural resources*, Concept Publishing Company, New Delhi, p.185.

Mukhopadhyay, Susmita et al., (2002): A study on gender differences in job satisfaction in an urban setting, *Journal of the Indian Anthropological Society*, 37(3): 287-291, November.

Muller, Sherin (1997): An analysis of the characteristics of women's groups and their role in Rural development, M.Sc. (Ag.) thesis, K.A.U. Thrissur.

NABARD, (1995): *As the Darkness Fades Away National Bank for Agricultural and Rural Development*, Trivandrum, p.8.

Nagayya, D. (2000): Micro finance for self-help groups, *Kurukshetra*, Vol.48, pp.10-12.

Nanjaiyan, K. (1985): Rationality in decision making by small farmers, Ph.D. thesis, TNAU, Coimbatore.

Reddy, N.G. (2001): *National conference on Self-help groups in the country and SGSY*: June 23-24, 2001, Background Material, NIRD.

Reddy, N.G. (2002): Empowering women through self-help groups and Micro credit: The case of NIRD Action Research projects, *Journal of Rural Development*, Vol.21, No.4, pp.551-535.

Narayana Swamy *et. al.*, (2003): Networking SHGs and cooperatives – an analysis of strengths and weaknesses, *Journal of Rural Development.*

Natarajan, L. (1998): *Haritha year – Kerala Calling 18* pp.2, Department of Public relations, Government of Kerala.

Nefa, V. and S. Someshwar (1998): DWCRA: Hope of light for women's development in rural areas, *Kurukshethra*, Vol-XLVI, No.7, 7-11 & 19.

Nelson, S. (1992): Role of Krishi Bhavan in Agricultural Development in Thiruvanthapuram District, M.Sc. (Ag.) thesis KAU, Thrissur.

NIRD, Hyderabad (2000-2001): *Access to credit for women Beneficiaries under SGSY*: Case study in Bidar District - Major findings.

Nirmala et al., (2004): SHGs for poverty alleviation in pondichery, *Journal of rural development*, NIRD, Hyderabad, Vol.23 (2).

Nizamudeen, A. (1996): A multidimensional Analysis of Kuttimulla cultivation in Alappuzha district, M.Sc., (Ag.) thesis, KAU, Thrissur.

O'Brien, P.J. (1997). Global processes and politics of sustainable development in Colombia and Costa Rica - Approaches to Sustainable Development, PINTER London: 169-193.

Oakley, P. *et al.*, (1992): *Projects with people: The practice of participation in Rural Development* (Geneva-International Labour Organization), pp.9-10.

Ojha, R.K. (2001): Self-help groups and rural employment, Yojana.

Osotimehin and Olawoye, Ibadan: ORG – MARG Research Limited women's Empowerment and Reproductive Health, Social Sciences and Reproductive Health Research Network.

Panda, A.K. and Mishra, A.K (1996): Informal co-operatives in Orissa-rediscovering cooperation (Ed, Rajagopaln, R.) Indian Institute of Management, Anand, Gujarat 2-216-235.

Pathak, P.A. (1992): Self-help groups and their linkages with banks. National Bank News Review, pp.9-10.

Patil (2002): Rural development programme; A study on women beneficiaries. *Indian Journal of Training and Development*, 32 (4), 89-90 October-December.

Pillai, Renuka and Lakshmi Devi, K.R. (2003): Influence of female earners on the economic status of the family: Some evidence from the micro level, *Asian Economic Review*, 45(1), 13-22.

Pitt, M. and Khandekar, S.R. (1998) : The impact of group-based credit programmes on poor households in Bangladesh; Does the gender of participant matter, *Journal of Political Economy*, 106(5) : 958-995.

Porchezian, M.R. (1991): An analysis of entrepreneurial behaviour of farmer, unpublished M.Sc. Agriculture thesis, TNAU, Coimbatore.

Prasad, C. (1995): Development of women and children in rural areas successful case studies, *Journal of Rural Development*, Vol.14(1), 66-87.

Prasad, C. (1995): Development of women and Children in Rural areas: Successful case studies, *Journal of Rural Development*, 14(1), p.65-87.

Puhazhendi and B, Jayaraman (1999) : Rural credit delivery; performance and challenges before Banks, *Economic and Political Weekly*, Jan., p.16-23.

Puroshotham, P. (2004). Marketing support to the SHGs, *Kurukshetra*, pp.23-28.

Puyalvannan, P. (2003): Micro-credit Innovations: A study basedon Microcredit, women empowerment and living of SHG with co-operative bankes in Tamil Nadu.

Rajakutty, S. (1994). A DWCRA Odyssey in North 24 paraganas – A learning experience, *Journal of Rural Development*, Vol.13, No.3, July-September.

Rajakutty, S. (1997): Development of women and children is rural areas (DWCRA), *Journal of Rural Development*, Vol.23(2).

Rajasekhar, D. (1993): Savings and credit systems of the poor as a strategy of economic development. Some NGDOs experiences paper presented at the Mid. Term review meeting of partners NGDOS of NOVIB. No.30 to Dec.4, 1993, Bangalore.

Rakesh Prasad, (2007): Information Support for empowerment in India, *Social Welfare*, April, 2007.

Rakowski, C. (1994) : Convergence and Divergence in informal sector debate. *World Development*, 22(4).

Ramachandran, C. (1992): Impact of Rice minikit trials on the adoption behaviour of farmers M.Sc. (Ag.) thesis, KAU, Thrissur.

Rangi, P.S. and others (2002): Economic empowerment of rural women through self-help groups: A case study of Fatehgarh Sahib district (Punjab), *Man and Development*, 24(3), 65-78, September.

Rao, D (1994); Self-help group and credit, *Arthavijnana* 36(3): 194-208.

Rao, M (1997): Development of women and children in rural areas – an appraisal. *Kurukshetra*, Vol.6, pp-46-49.

Rao, M.J. (1998) : DWCRA group of pallipadu shows the way, *Journal of Grameen Vikas*, Vol.4 (6), pp.13-25.

Rao, V. D. and B. Sarojani *et al.* (2005) : Evaluation studies, The Associate Publishers, Ambala Cantt, New Delhi.

Rao. V.M. (2002): Women Self-help groups profiles from Andhra Pradesh and Karnataka, *Kurukshethra*, Vol.VI, 29-31.

Rekha R. Gaonkar (2002): Role of SHGs in empowerment of women, Report on NIRD, Seminar, Hyderabad.

Rippen G. Jassal. (2007): Empowered women Nation's Strength, *Social Welfare Journal*, April, 2007.

Rizwana, A. (2002): Economic empowerment of women through women development corporations: *A Study of Maharastra Women Development Corporation.*

Rizwana, A. (2003): Economic empowerment of women through women development corporations: A study of Maharastra women Development Corporation, Hyderabad, NIRD (Case studies Series) -15.

Roul, S. (1996): *Cooperation, Indian Institute of Rural Management*, Anand, Gujarat, 2.249-269.

Roy Burman, J.J. (2002): A glimpse into self-help in tribal areas, *Journal of the Indian Anthropological Society*, 37(2), 113-121, July.

Sabya Sachidas (2003): Self help groups and micro credit synergic integration, *Kurukshethra*, Vol.IV, 26-27.

Sadamate, V.V. (1978): Globalisation of Indian Agriculture thoughts on Revamping Agricultural extension – Symposium.

Samantha, R.K (1977): A study on some agro-economic, socio-psychological and communication variables associated with repayment of Agricultural credit of Nationalised Bank, Ph.D. Thesis, Bidhen Chandra Krishi Viswa Vidyalaya Naida, West Bengal.

Santhanam, M.L. Singh, V. and Azad, G.S. (1990): Rural groups – a study of behavioural and interactional patterns, *Journal of Rural Development* 9(4): 703-770.

Sarada Devi, M. and Rayalu, T.R. (2002): Factors functioning in women empowerment in urban areas. *Journal of Community Guidance and Research*, 19(3), 339-351, November.

Seema, B. (1986): Role of farm women in decision making process of a farming community in Trivandrum District, M.Sc., (Ag.) Thesis, KAU, Thrissur.

Sen, Amartya (1999): *Women's Agency and Social Change*, in development as freedom.

Shankar Chattrjee (2004): Empowering women through microfinance, *Women's Link*, Vol.10, No.3-15.

Shanthi, T. (1996): Comparative analysis of characteristics of women labourers engaged in rice farming in the social system of Kollam and Kanyakumari District, Ph.D. thesis, KAU, Thrissur.

Shaw, V.S. (1993): Racial features and inference closes in interpersonal, person perception and inter personal behaviour, Stanford University Press.

Shishirkala, *et. al.*, (2001) : Economic viability of tribal women headed dairy enterprise : A case study, Bihar *Journal of Agricultural Marketing*, 9(2), 190-197, April-June.

Shubham Singh et al. (2003): Knowledge on basis of SHG: an exploratory survey in farm labour colonies, *Journal of Rural India* 69-71.

Shylendra, H.S. (1998) : Promoting women's Self-Help Groups - Lessons from an action research project of IRMA, Gujarat.

Sindhu, S. (1997): Prospects and constraints of commercial cut flower production in Thiruvananthapuram district, M.Sc. (Ag.) thesis, KAU, Thrissur.

Singh, A. (1995): NABARD-APARCA. International Seminar of development of rural poor through the self-help groups, May 29-30, Bangalore.

Sinha, A. (2004): Microfinance for women empowerment – A perspective, *Kurukshetra*, April, 2004, pp.31-38.

Sitalakshmi, S. et al., (1995): Dissemination of health messages to the beneficiaries of DWCRA programme. *Kurukshethra*, Vol.15, No.3, 87-90.

Sivaprasad, S. (1997): Problems and prospects of trained rural youth in agriculture, M.Sc. (Ag.) thesis, KAU, Thrissur.

Sood, A. (2004): Sustainable Rural development, *Kurukshetra*, April 2004, pp.27-30.

Sreedaya (2000) : Performance analysis of the self-help groups in vegetable production in Thiruvananthapuram district, M.Sc., Agriculture thesis.

Sreedharan, D. (1997) : Encourage self-help groups, *Social Welfare*, p.34.

Sudha Rani, K. (2005) : Influence of literacy and SHG participation on the awareness of development programmes, *Journal of Adult Education and Extension*, Vol.1, No. 2, p.39.

Sujit Kumar Paul (2004): Women empowerment through self-help groups, *Journal of Extension Research*, Vol.VI, 26-27.

Suneetha, R. (2007): Is DWCRA Programme Empowering the Rural Women, *Krukshethra*, Vol.55, March, 2007, p.17-18.

Surekha Rao, K. and Padmaja G. (1998): Self-help groups in Tirupati, Andhra Pradesh – *Journal of Social Welfare*, Vol.45, No.1, 25-27.

Tesoriero, F (2006) : Strengthening Communities through women's self help groups in South India, *Community Development Journal*, Vol.41, No.3 pp.321-333.

The South Malabar Gramin Bank (1998): *Monitoring study on SHGs.*

Thejaswini C.N. and Veerabhadraiah V. (1997) : Knowledge Assessment of rural women on DWCRA and their problems, *Kurukshetra*, Vol.XLV, No.10, pp.48-49.

Thomas J.A. (1998): *Family background, Education and Economic Success: A Hypothesis about the Determinants of Earning, Education and Economic Development*, Anmol Publications Pvt. Ltd., New Delhi.

Titus & Sebastin, A.P. (2001): Impact of microcredit programme of NGOs on Rural Women, *IASSI Quarterly*, 20(2) 135-142, October-December.

Tripathy, S.N. (2002): *Women in informal sector*, New Delhi, Discovery Publishing House, 108 p.

Udai Pareek, G. Trivedi (1964): *Manual of socio-economic status scale*, Manasayan Publishers, Delhi.

Uma Rameswary (1991): Women and Development, The *Indian Journal of Labour Economics*, Vol.34, No.4.

UNDP (1995): *Human Development Report*, New York, Oxford: Oxford University Press.

UNICEF, (1993): *The Women's Empowerment Framework Women and Girls Advance*, Vol.1, No.1, p.5.

Varma (2002) : Microfinance : "Emerging challenges" *Indian Journal of Public Administration*, Vol.XLVIII, No.2.

Vasudeva Rao, D. (2003) : Emerging leadership of women in Institutions of local governance : a study in Andhrapradesh, *Social Action*, 53(2), 59-1168, April-June.

Venkata Ravi, R. (2001): Growth patterns of Self-help groups in India, *Journal of SEDNE*, Vol.28, No.1, 18-25.

Williams, S. (1994): *The Oxfam Gender Training Manual.*

Yadagiri, K. (1996) : Rural poor and a challenging task of DWCRA : a study of women in Andhra Pradesh, *Journal of Southern Economics*, Vol.(5)34, pp.5-8.

Yadappanavar (1995): *Self-employment generation for women a DWCRA experiment in Karnataka*, Vol.34, No.5, 5-8.

Yerram Raju, B. and Firdausi (1997): Women's development issues, concerns and approaches, *Journal of Rural Development*, Vol.16(1), 25-27.

Yound, K. (1993): *Planning Development with women making a world of difference*, London, Macmillan.

Index